THE POPE AND THE NEW APOCALYPSE

The Holy War Against Family Planning

STEPHEN D. MUMFORD

Center for Research on Population and Security
Research Triangle Park, North Carolina   1986

Library of Congress Catalog Card Number: 86-70854
ISBN 0-937307-00-9 Hardcover
ISBN 0-937307-01-7 Paperback
Printed in the United States of America
First Printing, 1986
Second Printing, 1986
Third Printing, 1986

Cover Photo:
Reuters/Bettmann NewsPhotos

"We have in this country an admirable alternative
to civil war, and to holy civil war at that.
It's called the Constitution."

Bill Moyers   CBS News   September 12, 1984

Contents

Introduction

Under the headline, "The Pope and the President—Two of a Kind," syndicated columnist Jim Fain wrote last summer, "These are two marvelous old charmers, beguiling and impossible not to like, but they are downright dangerous on population control questions, and totally out of touch when it comes to the rights and role of women."[1]

At about the same time National Organization of Women president Eleanor Smeal, speaking at the National Press Club in Washington, said she intended to steer her organization toward political confrontation, and lead it "back to the streets" in a "mass mobilization" of activists to protect women's right to abortion—the right now protected by the 1973 U.S. Supreme Court decision on Roe vs. Wade.

Mrs. Smeal added emphatically, "The fight to outlaw abortion, and make no mistake about it, is an attack on birth control."[2] The Religious Coalition for Abortion Rights, representing major U.S. non-Catholic churches whose aggregate membership is 33 million, concurs: In a wrap-up titled "Family Planning: Going, Going, Gone?" the Coalition observed, "Using the abortion controversy as a smokescreen, opponents of family planning have scored partial victories that will greatly affect women and their families around the world."[3] The Coalition and others increasingly have noted that the abortion controversy is now threatening the basic principles of the United States Constitution.

Beneath the iceberg's tip

Last September, after the tragic earthquake devastated Mexico City, James Reston wrote in the *New York Times* about how such dramatic "accidents of life and death" called attention to Mexico's even more tragic population crisis. Washington has been so transfixed by conflicts with Moscow on such things as Star Wars, he wrote, "—It seems to have forgotten what was happening on its southern border in the night—namely, a population explosion, almost a dust of people fleeing from poverty across our borders, which are now beyond our control."[4]

Mr. Reston knows whereof he speaks. Mexico's impoverished men, women, and children are swarming across the Rio Grande into the U.S. in mounting numbers. Mexico began this century with a population of 10 million and is expected to end it with at least 100 million. This brings the world population dilemma close to home quite literally—as we see the pressure on our southern border in stark, heartrendingly human terms.

Though it is hard not to like Pope John Paul II and President Ronald Reagan, a backlash is beginning against their kinship on policies and programs related to population growth control and women's rights. It is a backlash against the manifest excesses of the Reagan Administration, the anti-abortion movement, and the Catholic Church in dealing with these contentious issues. It is drawing increasing attention from the mainstream press—not just the big city liberal papers that Spiro Agnew used to rail against—partly because grave Constitutional issues are involved. They include freedom of the press, freedom of speech, and the separation of church and state.

The backlash perhaps has been slow in coming, in part because of Americans' ingrained respect for religious freedom and civil rights. Not long ago, the *Syracuse Herald-Journal,* a sophisticated daily but not exactly a city slicker newspaper, put it this way: "Whether bullying in front of abortion clinics or barraging opponents with pieties, the religious right has learned to use its muscle. Many people are unwilling to argue back—to stand up for their point of view. They're intimidated by men and women of the cloth. It's alien to their upbringing to contradict a priest, minister or rabbi. Sometimes, though, people have to speak up—or be trampled by zealots from the left or right."[5]

The Syracuse editor was writing about "Bible Bigots," and of course many of the most vociferous among them are not Catholics but fundamentalist Protestants. In Congress and in the streets outside of abortion and birth control clinics, the Protestants are often the hit men. This practice protects the Catholic priesthood and the hierarchy from gross, unseemly involvement—in much the same way that these same Protestants, with the help of Presidential sidemen such as Messrs. Bennett and Meese, help preserve the famous teflon finish on President Reagan.

I haven't formed my own views on this subject from following the media, though I'm grateful for the growing media attention to this controversy. I have reached my own conclusions in ways I have been trained to do as a research scholar, and have devoted 15 years of painstaking research and analysis to this effort. In the main narrative of this book, for the most part I will present my facts and logic as dispassionately as possible. In this introduction, however, I'm allowing myself the luxury of some emotion—since I believe the welfare and future of mankind are at stake. They are threatened in ways which may become cataclysmic in our lifetime, indeed in ways which are causing grievous difficulty in parts of the world right now. Mainly my conclusions are these:

- The primary energy, organization, and direction of the anti-abortion, anti-family planning, anti-population-growth-control movement in the United States comes mainly from the hierarchy of the Roman Catholic Church, centered in Rome.
- The interests of the Vatican have superseded the best interests of the United States and the American people in matters concerning the dilemma of world population growth, and its relation to our national security.
- Though the non-Catholic wing of the misnamed "pro-life" movement has shown great expertise in the uses of single-issue politics and fundraising, it remains dependent for much of its energy and clout on the vast experience, organization and wealth of the Roman Catholic Church.
- The population dilemma, matched in urgency only by the possibility of nuclear war, is still the greatest threat to world peace and material improvement for most of the world's people.

- Though contraception as a means of limiting family size and population growth is doubtless preferable to abortion, voluntary abortion is still necessary in many developing countries as a fertility control measure, and will continue to be for some time.
- The Roman Catholic Church will stop at nothing within its power, quite literally I'm convinced, to impose its pro-natalist agenda on the American people and their government.
- If the destruction of U.S. Constitutional and representative democracy is found by the Vatican to be necessary to achieve its goals, the Church will not hesitate to attempt this.
- Indeed it is not hesitating to venture in this direction, because its hierarchy believes that the imposition of its will on the issue of population and family-planning is essential to the survival of the Church in its present, potent form.
- In the present U.S. political environment, the approaches of accommodation and dialog are manifestly inadequate to revitalize and accelerate U.S. family planning and population stabilization programs. Dialog alone has resulted in these programs being severely crippled and held captive. Therefore a sophisticated, integrated confrontational strategy is necessary.

It is not the purpose of this book to argue the urgency of dealing with the world population dilemma, or the essential humanity of extending safe and effective fertility control to men and women everywhere. That has been done by the best demographers, economists and medical and social scientists who have studied it, and by heads of state and other government leaders in a growing number of developing and developed countries alike.

Our concern in the United States for world population growth is not as great as it was two decades ago. One factor has been that the gradual spread of family planning in the developing world has created the impression that "the situation is well in hand," or at least is beginning to be so. The fact is that about two-thirds of the women in the developing world still have little or no access to modern family planning methods.

Another factor in the lack of concern is that most of us still don't grasp the quite unprecedented nature and truly awesome magnitude and tidal force of current world population increase. "No man is an island" which can escape the consequences of rampant population growth, though Americans may be sheltered temporarily from its ravages in distant lands.

As the simplest kind of backdrop for the narrative that follows, I am including a schematic view of the problem with this introduction. When you examine it, keep the following observation in mind: "The expected growth of world population, even according to minimum estimates, is of a kind that puts before humanity great problems, the like of which it has never known before. It can be said that the world population problem forms the first world problem in history . . . the implications of which are of direct importance to the welfare of universal humanity."[6]

That assessment was made not by a Malthusian true believer or birth control advocate but by the respected Catholic scholar, Professor George H. L. Zeegers, editor of the international journal of Catholic social scientists, *Cross Currents*, published in Geneva.

Readers need not accept all of my conclusions to be alarmed by the fabric of evidence that supports them. I hope they will respond by becoming part of the growing network that is beginning to give structure and thrust to the backlash against the increasingly menacing, implacable efforts of the Roman Catholic Church, with the Reagan Administration and the so-called pro-life movement as allies, to sabotage or terminate family planning programs.

Stephen D. Mumford
Chapel Hill, North Carolina
February, 1986

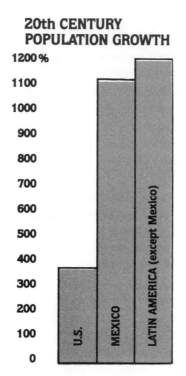

20th CENTURY POPULATION GROWTH

Percentage increases in population for the years 1900 to 2000, in the areas shown, based on actual increases to 1985, plus projected growth from 1985 to the year 2000. Sources: Population Reference Bureau and *Population*, Dennis Wrong, Random House.

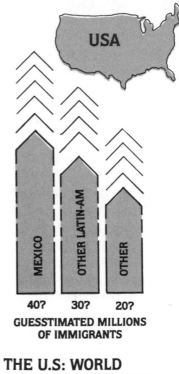

GUESSTIMATED MILLIONS OF IMMIGRANTS

THE U.S: WORLD IMMIGRATION TARGET

Guesstimates or informed guesses on influx of immigrants to the U.S. in the years 1975 to 2000.

PRESSURE FROM THE SOUTH

Population pressures are mounting throughout the Third World. For U.S. Citizens, the most striking example of this is just south of the border, as shown on the left above. The expected growth of Mexican population in the course of the 20th Century, from 10 million to 113 million, is an increase of 1,130 percent. In the same period, the rest of Latin America will have increased from 53 to an estimated 639 million, an astonishing 1,205 percent. Meanwhile, U.S. population will have grown from 71 million to a projected 268 million, up 377 percent. Current projections indicate that world population will have grown from 1.6 billion in the year 1900 to 6.1 billion before this century ends. It is generally acknowledged that the tide of illegal immigration into the U.S. has risen swiftly, with private studies indicating 12–20 million illegal immigrants entering our country by 1984. "Guesstimates" of projected legal plus illegal immigration, mainly the latter, are depicted to the end of the century, on the right. These guesstimates assume that rapid population growth will continue in the next decade, along with Vatican efforts to frustrate both fertility control and immigration control.

Of Democracy and Population

From the pinnacle of the electronic ministry, the Rev. Pat Robertson said in 1979, "I'd like to see evangelicals get back into this [political] area of life . . . We should get involved in the political process . . . If you put the Catholics and the evangelicals together, it is a clear majority."[7] And in 1984, the People For The American Way's "televangelist summary" reported Robertson as saying, "There is nothing in the Constitution that sanctifies the separation of church and state."[8] Incredible!

Of course it is unlikely that Catholics and evangelicals form a clear majority of U.S. church goers, much less of adult Americans generally. They don't even come close if Catholics who condone and indeed practice artificial contraception and abortion are excluded. But that kind of numbers game is beside the point. The Constitution does indeed protect religious freedom and religious minorities, as well as church-state separation. Today there are many points at which the cabal of radical right fundamentalists, the Catholic Church establishment, and the Reagan Administration are tinkering with Constitutional fundamentals.

As Anthony Lewis wrote last year, "The Reagan Administration has already indicated that correct views on abortion [or fetal personhood theology] are to be a standard for judicial appointees. To demand belief in a particular doctrine—to demand it of judges or candidates for President—is as profoundly wrong as it would be to demand membership in a particular denomination. The framers of our Constitution wrote in Article VI: *'No religious test shall ever be required as a qualification for any office or public trust under the United States.'*"[9]

Yet belief in "fetal personhood theology" is a religious test, a theology not accepted by the vast majority of Protestants in America. In part, this is because of reasons described by Presbyterian minister, John H. Galbreath in Appendix 1.

Meanwhile, it is well recognized that such things as last year's Kemp-Hatch proposal to deny Federal support to family planning clinics providing abortion counseling is a clear offense to medical ethics. More importantly here, however, as Suzanne Lynn of the American Civil Liberties Union pointed out, "it offends the Constitution as well."[10] In violating the First Amendment's guarantee of free speech, she notes, "A more blatantly unconstitutional condition would be hard to envision." There is a special irony here also that the U. S. Agency for International Development last fall granted a special, highly irregular, guarantee of free speech to those who counsel only natural family planning, which has depended mainly on the Catholic-approved "rhythm method." With this pro-Catholic ploy, Lynn points out, the federal government is in effect funding the teaching of religious dogma—in direct violation of the Constitution's guarantee of separation of church and state.

The breadth of the attack of the Reagan Administration on the Constitution is increasingly evident. Education Secretary William Bennett has charged that the Supreme Court failed to recognize Judeo-Christian values when it upheld a recent ruling that limited aid to parochial schools.

At nearly the same time, Attorney General Edwin Meese, III, began pressing his case that the Supreme Court frequently fails to abide by the intent of the Constitution's framers. Thus began an extraordinary debate in which some Supreme Court justices felt impelled to publicly defend the workings and decisions of their body, and to question the recollections about judicial history on which Mr. Meese relied in his attack. Is the concentration of Catholic cabinet members in the present Administration, and their blitz of Constitutional questions, simply a matter of a strong leader bringing vigorous, like-minded lieutenants onto his team—or is it something more, and perhaps something less wholesome or democratic?

The policy role reversal

The anti-family planning assault entered a new phase in the summer of 1984. The consequences of this are still unfolding. The shot heard 'round the world on population policy was the position taken by the U.S. government delegation to the U. N. Population Conference in Mexico City. This has been exhaustively analysed, with ample press coverage, and requires only brief comment here.

In essence, with direction from the White House, the U.S. began to shift away from fairly full-fledged support of overseas family planning programs. It did so by strengthening Administration opposition to those programs which provided or counseled abortion, and by advancing what might be called a "supply side" theory of the relationship between human fertility decline and economic development. The primary architect of this was University of Maryland teacher Julian Simon.

The gist of the new policy thrust, as just about everyone now knows, is that the key to slowing population growth in developing countries is deregulation and the unleashing of "free market" forces. In other words, with the working of free markets among nations released from the thrall of Communism, fertility decline would promptly follow economic development. Coupled with this was the truism that people are "the ultimate resource;" they are producers as well as consumers; and therefore population growth should stimulate both production and consumption. At least in free market economies.

There are rich ironies here. At the first U.N. Population Conference in Bucharest ten years earlier, the rallying cry of many Third World representatives was that "development is the best contraceptive." U.S. delegates contrarily argued that although fertility decline historically did follow economic development, the population vs. resources crisis, and the grinding poverty and political unrest among many less developed nations, does not allow time for this slow decline to occur—and, in fact, economic development is substantially dependent on curbing population growth.

But now in Mexico City, the positions were reversed. In the Worldwatch Institute's latest *State of the World* report, this recap is given: "At Mexico City, at times the only dissenting voice was that of the United

States. Among developing nations, a new tone of urgency could be heard . . . No longer was it a matter of whether there was a need to slow population growth. The question was how: Which contraceptives were most effective and how could they be delivered to people who needed them? And further, how can smaller families be encouraged?"[11]

Beyond the irony of the reversal of positions between the developing nations and the United States in the decade before the Mexico City conference, is another, imbedded in the position taken by the U.S. delegation: As ecologist Lester Brown comments, "Those preparing the [U.S.] statement apparently overlooked China's success in bringing down population growth within an economic environment that has anything but free enterprise. They also conveniently ignored the fact that the country with the lowest birth rate in the Western Hemisphere, lower even than the United States, is Cuba, a centrally planned economy."[12]

In fact, because of the aggressive way in which China has pushed ahead with its fertility control program, more than half of the Third World's family planning users are in that country—with its population in excess of one billion. While the average woman in China gives birth to two children, the average for other developing countries is five.

So while Professor Simon and the Reagan Administration highlight the spread of family planning in the Third World, they gloss over the magnitude of China's contribution to this—a contribution still dependent heavily on the practice of abortion. Surely I find coercive abortion as repugnant as anyone, but again this is not the point. The point simply is that the Administration's selective use of data on the relationship between free market economies and fertility decline yields a case that is false—false according to any scholarly test, or the test of experience in Third World countries, whatever their economies may be.

The consensus electrified

Within the broad coalition that long ago recognized how uncurbed fertility would inevitably devastate the well-being of both families and nations, the new U.S. population policy presented in Mexico City came as a form of electric shock therapy. Perhaps it was needed to galvanize the coalition anew, since a certain self-satisfaction had resulted from its moderate but measurable gains.

The backlash against the Vatican-supported Administration policy began building even before it was officially unveiled at the UN conference.

One vigorous spokesman has been retired World Bank president Robert McNamara—very much a "bottom line"-oriented person. In response to the Simonesque assertion that world population growth has ceased to be a pressing problem, Mr. McNamara shunned elegance to say, "That's a bunch of crap."[13] In an article published in *Foreign Affairs*, he argued that the population bomb is just as explosive as ever.

Though recognizing that the rate of world population growth has declined slightly, McNamara pointed out a disturbing fact: The fall-off has come almost exclusively in the developed world, while birth rates in most developing countries are as high, or nearly as high, as ever. Within the next century, India's population is projected to climb from 675 million to 1.6 billion, Nigeria's from 85 million to more than 500 million, and El Salvador's from 5 million to 15 million. Worldwide, that would add up to a total of 11 billion before population stabilizes—more than double its present figure.

Long before that, dire consequences would spread like an atomic cloud: Third World families would be driven to unprecedented levels of abortion and infanticide—particularly of female babies. Developing countries would be left with massive unemployment, hideously sprawling cities, woefully inadequate food supplies, ravaged environments, and a continuing escalation of what McNamara terms "absolute poverty"—that is, living conditions "so characterized by malnutrition, illiteracy and disease as to be beneath any reasonable definition of human decency."[14] A rash of political upheavals in Third World countries would be a predictable corollary of this.

Robert McNamara is a realist and accepts the sad truth that reality is where most of us live. And die. A growing number of Catholics, from bankers and corporate CEOs to feminist nuns, also accept this fact. When the spunky group, Catholics for a Free Choice, asserted that, "A diversity of opinions regarding abortion exists among committed Catholics,"[15] Jean Jerome Cardinal Hamer, head of the Vatican's Congregation for Religious and Secular Institutes replied, "The radical immorality of direct abortion is clear, constant, and unequivocal."[16]

Cardinal Hamer warned that the 24 nuns who backed the CFC position would be dismissed from their religious orders if they failed to recant. CFC director Frances Kissling commented, "Cardinal Hamer is totally unaware of the nature of political life in America. The values of free speech are just not understood,"[17] in the cloistered Vatican. There is an inescapable parallelism between the Cardinal's insensitivity to the democratic process and the attacks on the Constitution that have become part of the Reagan Administration's second term agenda.

Another troubling phenomenon is part of this dynamics. Even with the new energy and potential broadening of the coalition favoring worldwide family planning and recognizing the gravity of the population crisis, a curious anomaly remains: On the one hand, Catholic and non-Catholic advocates of broad family planning programs and world population growth control are fighting side by side for these convictions and arguing their case publicly, to the extent of spot-lighting the intrusion of the Vatican into the functioning of democracy. On the other hand, many others who share these beliefs remain "in the closet."

Why? Recently a friend of mine attended a strategy meeting of family planning, population and health professionals who are seeking new approaches to countering the losses and threats their cause has suffered under the Reagan Administration. My friend said that another participant in the meeting commented, "We must find ways to explore and expose the pro-lifers: Who are they? What are their motives? What powers are behind them? Where does their money come from? These are the central issues." My friend asked, "Have you or your organization asked these blunt questions publicly?" The reply was that they had not, and could not—not yet. My friend told me, "If we remain in the closet much longer, we will be buried there." Of course I cannot reveal my friend's name.

This is not simply ironic, it's pathetic. Yet understandable: Most professionals in family planning and allied fields are past or present beneficiaries of federal investment in their programs. Even beyond the deeply ingrained respect of Americans for religious and civil liberties, they know they are at risk in the present political environment. They quite understand the power of reprisal of the Catholic Church and the power of money in the U. S. Treasury—the power to give and to take away, and as a reward for good behavior sometimes to give a little bit back. The disciplinary power of the Church exhibited in the case of the 24 nuns who signed the freedom of belief on abortion statement is kid stuff, compared to other actions the Church has taken to impose its will. At any rate that is the pained conviction of Catholic priests and scholars of tested integrity who have left the fold to spill the beans.

The New Apocalypse

When Pope John Paul II visits other lands, his tour is an event attracting media coverage second only to the travels of President Reagan. Both men are caring, articulate and warm. They are charismatic and photogenic. As the Pope moves from place to place, what do we see on our television screens and read in our papers? And what are the back-drops of the human situation, sometimes just beyond camera range, that are the contexts of the Pope's journeys?

The Pope visits Latin America, and walks among its people. We see the Pope in Rio, speaking to a throng of faithful in the slums. And beyond the crowd, whether we can glimpse them or not, are the aban-doned children, living unkempt and hungry in the streets, scavenging in garbage to survive.

The Pope speaks against contraception, and praises the blessings of new life. In Brazil, the population growth rate is 2.3 percent a year —compared to the world population growth rate of 1.7. Brazil's 138.4 million population in 1985 is expected to double in 30 years. Brazil is suffering a severe economic recession, chronic and acute unemployment, and its foreign debt is the largest in the world. Brazil's predicament is only slightly better or slightly worse than that of most other Latin American countries.

The Pope visits Africa and walks among its people. In Zaire, he speaks out against exploitation of the poor, apartheid, and the repression of political dissent. We see him graciously accepting the gift of a handkerchief from an awed, beautiful Zairean Girl Scout, at the Notre Dame Cathedral in Kinshasa. The annual population growth rate in Zaire is 2.9 percent; the nation's population is expected to double in the next 24 years.

In Cameroon, the Pope acknowledges "the grave problems posed by population growth in some parts of the world."[18] But he repeats the Roman Catholic Church's opposition to contraception and all policies of "anti-life," urging Africans to resist Western-sponsored birth control efforts.[19] Cameroon's population growth rate is 2.6 percent annually. This will double human numbers there in 27 years.

In Kenya, the Pope confers with Cardinal Maurice Otunga, the Roman Catholic Archbishop of Nairobi, who has often spoken against birth control. But Kenya's president Daniel arap Moi has called openly on the people to have fewer children and to practice family planning, as an aid to family health and national progress. Kenya has the world's highest population growth rate—4.1 percent, expected to double Kenyan numbers in 17 years. Elsewhere in Africa, starvation spreads through Ethiopia and Sudan. In South Africa, ironically and tragically, population growth and population pressure on the white minority is a root cause of the repressive policies of apartheid that the Pope decries. In the African continent overall, the population is growing at the rate of 3 percent a year, faster than any other region. At that pace it will double in just 24 years.

Dogma vs change

One strength of any great religion is that it gives its believers the courage and faith to endure the inflictions of an often cruel fate, during the course of life. Surely Christianity, in both its Catholic and Protestant modes, has done that. Another strength of religion is that it affords anchors of stability in a changing, often chaotic, world, and may help its people prevail over the cruel caprice or excesses of their rulers. Christians have exercised this strength nobly. The other side of this second strength, however, is that church stability may congeal into concrete, so that church leaders rely on dogma so inflexibly that they simply institutionalize, and even sanctify, cultural lag.

Certainly our present world is chaotic enough. But the unprecedented nature of the population dilemma is bound to make it more so, in ways that even the most comfortable among us cannot escape—unless we move much more swiftly to help curb population growth.

In the midst of turmoil and change, we all seek leaders who give us hope. Hope and optimism may be found in fiction if not in fact. There has always been a bond between the theater and religion, and as economist and cultural historian John Kenneth Galbraith said recently, "Mr. Reagan is our first President from our theatrical tradition, and he is from its most impressively American form, the motion picture. In this tradition one does not ask whether the script conforms to reality; that is a denial of the art. The script has an imaginative dimension of its own; the script *is* the reality.

"So, inevitably, after a lifetime in this tradition, it is for Ronald Reagan . . . In consequence, no one should suppose that his observations should be expected to conform to fact. That would be a denial of his art. Accordingly, it is natural and even inevitable that the President should call the South African government reformist in intent; or say that segregation there has disappeared; or assert that the market will solve all problems including population control and farm distress in Iowa."[20]

Obviously, President Reagan believes what he says, or he could not say it so convincingly. His ebullient good humor stems, or at least gains substantial nourishment, from his belief in the imagined world of his script, not from the harsh realm of reality—the realm in which the rest of us are forced to reside. We have discovered, for example, that one cannot, for very long, have one's cake and eat it too; that one cannot have all those guns and all that butter, and at the same time reduce the national debt.

Pope John Paul II has his script as well—the dogma of his church. As with our President, some particulars of his script do not mix well with reality, such as his church's proscription on the "artificial" control of fertility. But his total belief in his script, in his dogma, is what columnist Fain would call part of his charm.

Conscience and survival

In 1963, in his book *The Time Has Come*, devout Catholic physician John Rock, co-developer of the birth control pill, wrote the following:

"When Christ walked among men, world population had reached an estimated 250 million. Even with this sizable number, the human race was still far from secure as a species. The Apocalyptic horsemen of famine and pestilence cast dread shadows over whole nations at a time. Every family was keenly aware of the hovering hand of death over each new infant, over each man and wife; the elderly were treated with special respect not alone for their wisdom but perhaps because they were so scarce. Life expectancy was of the order of twenty-five years. Respect for the admonition 'be fruitful and multiply' reflected man's knowledge of his precarious tenure in those days. The only defense against the slashing mortality that beset him was his own fertility."[21]

It was in this era that Catholic doctrine opposing fertility control began to evolve. In the Book of Revelation, St. John's vision of the Apocalypse symbolized the life of the Church in a hostile world and prophesied doom—the end of our material existence in a final act of God's wrath. But as Dr. Rock observes, mankind's demise was not delivered by the Apocalyptic horsemen, because biological science and a host of other developments came to the rescue. Today the threat to mankind may be measured in terms of not too few people, but too many. The world has changed in a fundamental, unforeseen way, but Roman Catholic doctrine has made no adjustment to this.

In consequence, Catholic dogma and authority, as expressed and symbolized by the Pope, threaten both the future of mankind and at present our own national security. Remember that Robert McNamara served perhaps his most difficult years as U. S. Secretary of Defense and is conditioned to keep our national security very much in mind.

Where would the present struggle of so many nations to curb their population growth be today if our present and recent popes had boldly led toward a change of Catholic doctrine—so that this great church could apply its power and wealth to helping families and nations curb their fertility, instead of insisting blindly on its suicidal increase? There was a moment, a quivering moment, during the Ecumenical Council and the papacy of John XXIII at the turn of the 1960's, when it looked as if Catholic doctrinal change toward a more affirmative position on population control and contraception might come to pass.

But John XXIII did not live long enough to help see this through, and since then Vatican intransigence has become increasingly shrill. As a result, John Paul II has a legacy, it seems to me, of bearing the burden of a looming New Apocalypse, one that threatens mankind not through

God's vengeance, but in large measure through Vatican failure to adjust and refine Catholic dogma in recognition of a fundamental new reality in the world: the quite unprecedented growth of human population. If this growth continues, humanity will be decimated, as more people compete for dwindling essential resources, by the original apocalyptic horsemen of famine, pestilence, war and death. Other churches have adjusted to the reality of growing population pressures in ways that strengthen, rather than weaken, their basic moral values.

Indeed, what *is* true morality in a changed and changing world, and where does it reside? In the preface to his book, John Rock talks about a conversation he had at the age of 14 with his parish priest, Father Finnick. He was riding in the priest's buggy, as the Father went to make a parish call, and they talked about the formation of conscience. The priest said, "John, always stick to your conscience. Never let anyone else keep it for you." Father Finnick paused and added, "And I mean *anyone else.*"[22]

John Rock was a loyal, loving Catholic who nonetheless dared to take issue with his Church when its dogma no longer reflected or addressed the realities he perceived in the world, as a scientist and sensitive observer of the human condition. And when his conscience told him that Catholic dogma on birth control was obstructing, not serving, true morality, he spoke out. For the most part, the Church seemed to treat his deviance with toleration. In another era, scholars and scientists whose new constructs of reality were found to be divergent from Catholic dogma were less fortunate. During the Inquisition, Bruno was burned at the stake for espousing the Copernican heresy that the earth revolved around the sun, and Galileo spent the last eight years of his life under house arrest for proving this to be so.

It would appear that in the four centuries from Galileo to John Rock, the Church has progressed. Yet the Vatican mindset that sought to stifle the Renaissance has changed little. To most of those at the center of Catholic power today, dogma is the ordering force of phenomena, not the other way around: to them, belief *confers* and filters reality.

An educational psychologist observing a child grappling with "The Three R's" the way the Vatican twists its way around the population crisis could easily conclude that the youngster has "a learning difficulty." A psychotherapist observing an adult with these symptoms might speak of "personality disorder." It is not hyperbolic to suggest that in the broad realm of sexuality, reproduction and the role and rights of women,

Vatican thinking is rather sick. Sympathetic though we may be to the mental illness of these cloistered males, the world should not have to suffer the consequences of their impairment.

Two ways to draw a horse

The current relationship between the powers of the Vatican and the Presidency of the United States has been called "an unholy alliance" formed to cripple if not destroy international efforts to curb population growth. I have called this relationship a cabal. Does it also constitute a conspiracy to undermine democracy in the United States? I simply pose the question. As you read this booklet, think about the musings of the late Senator Sam Ervin of North Carolina a few years ago, as he reminisced about Watergate. He was asked why the Watergate Committee he chaired did not attempt to deduce the guilt of particular individuals.

Senator Sam replied, "I think we found out exactly what Watergate was all about . . . There are two ways to draw a picture of a horse: One, you can draw a very good likeness of a horse, and all intelligent people can look at the picture and tell it's a horse. But if some people are not intelligent, it may be necessary not only to draw the picture, but to write under it, 'This is a picture of a horse.' We thought the American people were intelligent enough to know a horse when they saw its picture."[23]

Whether or not the alliance I describe here amounts to a conspiracy or is simply the fateful convergence of political and religious forces, the result is world threatening. Columnist Fain concludes his brief essay about "The Pope and the President" like this: "There's nothing to do about it except meet it head-on, all you tired liberals. Sorry to intrude on your nap, but some problems don't age well. It's time to take on these old matinee idols, however amiable, well-intentioned and difficult to counter they may be."[24] Amen.

Vatican Takeover

Following the death of the Simpson/Mazzoli Immigration Reform Bill, designed to limit illegal immigration into the United States and set a ceiling on legal immigration, on October 11, 1984,[25] a group of workers was discussing the demise of the bill. "What went wrong? Why were we defeated? We believed we had covered all the issues. We know a majority of the Senate and a majority of the House were in favor of the Senate version of the Bill. We know that 75% of the Hispanics were for employer sanctions and for an unforgeable social security card; among Blacks, 66% were for employer sanctions and 69% were for stepped-up control;[26] and that in 1977 and 1980 Roper polls 91% of the American people voted that they wanted all illegal immigration into the United States stopped."[27]

Privately, one of the group told me, "What went wrong is really a rhetorical question. Obviously, at least one thing that went wrong is that not one of the population groups in the United States, those good folks in the population establishment, has had the courage to identify and challenge the obvious enemy—that is, the political Roman Catholic Church—more specifically the Vatican Curia. Until they do, further defeats of any really substantial efforts to control immigration almost certainly will follow."

Conflict of interest

The political Vatican Curia must be distinguished from the religious, spiritual Church—the Holy See. Both Catholic Clergy[28] and Catholic laymen[29] have stated that the political Catholic Church often acts at the expense of the religious Catholic Church. The political Church sometimes hides under the skirts of the religious Church. It uses the religious Church to achieve political and economic goals which are sometimes clearly not in the best interests of the country concerned.

In 1980, Jean-Guy Vaillancourt, a Canadian Roman Catholic professor of sociology at the University of Montreal, published a book titled *Papal Power: A Study of Vatican Control Over Lay Catholic Elites* (Berkeley: University of California Press). Vaillancourt states,

> "In spite of the purely religious image that it endeavors to put forward, the Vatican is deeply involved in Italian and international politics and finance, promoting conservatism and capitalism while professing a Christian approach to democratic reforms. The Vatican is constantly intervening in Italian politics to protect its interests, including its economic interests. The Vatican is not only a political and a religious entity; it is also an important financial enterprise."

Certainly, no other church is so influential, or as opposed to birth control and restraints on immigration across U.S. borders as the Vatican. The best interests of the Vatican and the best interests of the United States are not always the same. Nowhere is this conflict more evident than in their responses to population growth in the U.S. and the world.

The solutions to world overpopulation—modern methods of contraception, voluntary sterilization, abortion as a backstop for contraception, illegal immigration control, expanding opportunities for women, sex education, incentives and disincentives for no more than two children—are, I am convinced, grave threats to the survival of the power of the Vatican, at least in its political dimension. Once these solutions have become the law of the land and are integral parts of public policy, the Vatican leadership believes they will seriously undermine the authority of the Church over its communicants. It is from this authority that the Vatican's political power is drawn. (For a more complete description of the ways in which Vatican power is threatened by population growth control, please see Appendix 2.)

According to Father Andrew Greeley, Vatican leaders are concerned not so much with the religious aspect of the Church as with its worldwide political power. States Greeley, "This sort of religion is the traditional concern of the Roman Curia, it always has been since the temporal power of the pope began . . . They are concerned about politics, administration, and finance."[30] The greater the number of their communicants, the greater the power of the hierarchy. These prelates, recognizing their jeopardy, have placed the religious dimension of the Church at risk in order to prevail politically — at least it appears that way to many observers inside and outside of the Catholic establishment.

Why overpopulation threatens national security

The United States National Security Council in 1979[31] and 1980[32] determined that severe pressures on land, water and air caused by current rates of world population growth seriously threaten the security of all nations, including the United States. The 1979 report concludes, "Much is being done, but the situation requires a major and urgent expansion of effort, if the world is to be spared *unprecedented deprivation and turmoil.*"

The threat to the United States is two-fold: internal and external. Internally, a 0.7% natural growth rate of 1.7 million enlarged by an unreported 0.8% immigration rate of 2 million (1.4 million illegal,[33] 0.6 million legal[34]) for a total growth of 3.7 million in 1984 would increase the current 236 million U.S. population to more than 300 million by the year 2000 if these rates continued. The resulting densities would exceed the carrying capacity of resources in most areas, increase unemployment with the advent of automation, cybernetics and robotics, along with almost surely increasing inflation, taxes and regulation; all of which predictably would increase poverty and cause social instability and strife within our own country.

Externally, the realistic possibility that unemployment and hunger may cause widespread disruption of social organization makes world population growth a serious national security issue, according to Ambassador Marshall Green.[35] Current examples are the overpopulated countries of the Middle East, including Egypt, Lebanon, Israel, Iraq and Iran and the overpopulated countries of Central America, including Mexico, Guatemala, El Salvador, Nicaragua and Honduras, the Middle East having an unsustainable average growth rate of 2.9% and Central America 2.7%.[36] Unless these growth rates can be stabilized and substantially reduced, no amount of U.S. military and economic aid can be expected to bring peace to the Middle East or Central America.

One serious study has produced a crude estimate of the number of aliens who will attempt illegal entry into the United States between 1980 and 2000 from all sources at 161 million.[37] This estimate was made through a country by country assessment of the number each country was expected to send. All parameters and assumptions used are discussed in detail in this study published in 1981 and their reasonableness has not been effectively disputed. Mind-boggling though it is, it is a solid fact that there are 0.5 billion U.S. border crossings annually by aliens: tourists, students, temporary workers and others.[38] If just 1.6% of this number chose to attempt to stay in the U.S. as illegal aliens, that would not be surprising. And if this number did stay, then 161 million people would have attempted to become illegal aliens between 1980 and the year 2000. If just half as many were successful in remaining, it would surpass the "invasion of the barbarians" which destroyed the Roman Empire. Even according to the most conservative figures, the illegal human tide of U.S. border crossings is rising undeniably. Apprehensions of illegal aliens in the Chula Vista border sector just south of San Diego have increased in the last 20 years from 6,000 per year to 407,000 per year."[39]

It is demonstrable that crowding brought on by overpopulation has long been an underlying cause of war. Recent examples from World War II are Germany and Japan. A chapter in Hitler's "Mein Kampf" is devoted to explaining the need of the German people for greater "Lebensraum" (Living Space). The square mile area of the five main islands of Japan and of California is equal, each with a mountain range running through them. In 1940, the population of Japan numbered 72 million, California 7 million. To justify Japan's aggression throughout Asia and the Pacific, Japanese apologists have asked what Californians might have done if their populations four decades ago had been reversed. By 1984, Japan's population had grown to 120 million and California's to 25 million. Though Japan is now a strong U.S. ally, it is struggling to support its further enlarged population by waging what has been called "economic warfare" against Europe and North America.

Thus the dimensions of the conflict are defined. The political Catholic Church (the Vatican) is pitted against the national security interests of the United States. Clearly, to ignore the overpopulation problem outside and within our borders, fostered and aggravated by the Vatican, will be to invite severe consequences and, ultimately, a severe undermining of our national security.

Politics and Catholic power

That the Vatican views the solutions to the population problem as threats to its authority over its communicants, and thus its political power, is well supported. Thomas Burch, one of the 64 lay members of the Papal Commission on Population and Birth Control (1966), recently revealed in the *National Catholic Reporter* that the tacit purpose of the Commission was to find a way for the Church to approve contraception without undermining Church authority.[40] So surely the Church is, or was, aware of its own dilemma. At the time, Burch was on the faculty of Georgetown University, and today is chairman of The University of Western Ontario's Department of Sociology. In the recent article cited, Burch said:

"Cardinal (John) Heenan (of Westminister, England) announced that it was the wish of 'the high authority' that we consider two propositions during the day.

"First proposition: suppose the Vatican changed its mind on contraception. What can we do to present this in such a way that the church will not lose its moral influence over people?

"Second proposition: Suppóse the Vatican does not change its mind on these issues. How can we preserve our (the church's) influence over the marital behavior of individuals?

"I think my very strong reaction was, 'What the heck's going on here? You are saying that you might have been wrong for nigh on 30 to 40 years on some details about methods; you've caused millions of people untold agony and unwanted children; brought on stresses and strains and tremendous feelings of guilt. You've told people they were going to hell because they wouldn't stop using condoms, and now you're saying maybe you're wrong? But you want to say it in such a way that you can continue to tell people what to do in bed?'

"I think at that point, the absurdity became very clear. My feeling was that what the church was most concerned with was exerting its own authority. It was not terribly concerned with human beings at some level."

Thus, the Vatican's position on population growth control and family planning is reduced to a question of authority, the control of individuals; it is reduced to a question of power—political power.

The Commission voted 64 to 4 that a change in the Church's stand on artificial birth control was both possible and advisable. The report had to be submitted in mid-1966 to a smaller commission of twenty cardinals and bishops, and that's where the crunch came. Obliged to record their own views of the report, six of the prelates abstained, eight voted in favor of recommending the report to the Pope, and six voted against it (including Pope John Paul II, then a Cardinal).[41]

This small minority vote was sufficient to enable Cardinal Alfredo Ottaviani, the prefect of the Holy Office, room to maneuver. Ottaviani was the most powerful person in the Roman Catholic Church next to the Pope and a bitter opponent of the liberalizing aspects of Vatican Council II. These few negative votes allowed the Cardinal to rally the old guard and throughout 1967 and early 1968 bring sufficient pressure on the Pope so that he ignored the advice of the Commission and published *Humanae Vitae* on July 25, 1968,[42] retaining the ban on so-called 'artificial contraception'. The powers of the Curia obviously had decided that the Vatican could not change its position without losing much or all of its political power.[43]

Humanae Vitae was an admission by the Vatican that the solutions to the population problem—modern methods of contraception, abortion, sterilization, expanding opportunities for women, sex education and the like—are in fact gravely threatening the survival of the Vatican, at least its political dimension, because they all undermine its authority.

For all practical purposes, therefore, Humanae Vitae was a declaration of a "holy war" against family planning and population growth control. Recognizing their jeopardy, the prelates placed the religious dimension of the Church at risk in order to prevail politically. The encyclical seriously divided the Church. On a disaster scale for the Roman Catholic Church it measures higher than the treatment of Galileo in the seventeenth century or the declaration of papal infallibility by Pius IX in 1870. This document, which was intended to strengthen papal authority, had precisely the opposite effect.[44]

From its perspective, the Vatican's actions are not as unreasonable as would appear on the surface. Illegal birth control and abortion, for example, are no threat to Vatican survival because, being illegal, they do not weaken Church authority. Their illegality means that civil authority is not pitted against Church authority—Church/State confrontation is avoided. *Between 7 and 12 million abortions are performed illegally in Catholic Latin America each year.*[45] The Church makes no attempt to stop them. Illegal abortion does not threaten their authority. The lives of thousands of women in those Roman Catholic countries who die from illegal abortion each year and the suffering of millions of others who survive apparently is a small price to pay to maintain Church authority.

Sadly, the institution of the Roman Catholic Church appears to have become a political one above all else. To survive and expand for so many centuries it was compelled to become a political power, and it has become a financial power as well. Sometimes the Church undertakes activities that are political or economic under the guise of religion. Menaced by public population policy in the U.S., which legally sanctions birth control, sex education, abortion and family size limitation, the Vatican is resorting to desperate and bold political measures here.

In his book, *American Freedom and Catholic Power* (The Beacon Press, 1949), Protestant minister, lawyer, and former State Department official, Paul Blanshard discussed what theoretically could happen to American democracy if the Catholic Church conducted itself as it had in most other countries in recent history, skillfully manipulating governments. He recognized that the Vatican and the U.S. at times do have conflicting interests, such as birth control. A person cannot always be loyal to the Pope and to the United States at once. When interests clash, choices must be made. Blanshard's book was labeled heretical and rabidly anti-Catholic by the Church. Librarians were ordered to remove it from their shelves.

The Holy War on Family Planning

In 1975 the National Conference of Catholic Bishops formulated and published for internal Church use the "Pastoral Plan for Pro-Life Activities." This Plan can be found in Appendix 3. The plan is directed toward creating a highly sophisticated, meticulously organized and well financed local, state and national political machine. In 1980, the Vatican went to great lengths to assist in the election of an American president, using the infrastructure created in accord with the Plan. Though the plan says that this political machine was created to combat legalized abortion, it has become obvious during the Reagan administration that the issue of abortion is simply a clever pretext for building a political machine designed to impose a much broader Vatican political agenda on the American people.

The plan frankly states that the Church will undertake activities to elect officials from local to national levels who will adhere to Vatican-ordained positions; that it will seek to influence policy in ways that will eliminate the threat to the Church; and that it will encourage the Executive Branch to deal "administratively" with matters that are unfavorable to the Church.

Starting with Parish, Diocesan, and State Coordinating Pro-Life Committees, the Plan concentrates on organizing all 435 Congressional Districts in the 50 states. The plan blue-prints in detail how each congressional district machine will be organized, how it will operate, what it will do and how it will respond to the National Conference of Catholic Bishops.

Pro-life does the dirty work

The Plan's implementers found a ready-made ally in Jerry Falwell. Falwell fits perfectly into the Catholic strategy of using non-Catholics where possible to serve as front men with the public. Falwell's Protestant constituency has been of enormous help, unwittingly, to the Bishops in moving toward the Pastoral Plan's objectives. In return, the Bishops generously supported the Moral Majority and Falwell financially, particularly after he agreed to emphasize abortion, in which, according to investigative reporter Connie Paige in her book "The Right to Lifers" (Summit Books, 1983), he previously had evidenced no interest.[46]

In effect, the finding that Catholic energy, organization and direction were essential to the right-to-life movement was foreshadowed by Federal Judge John J. Dooling in his 1980 decision on the Hyde Amendment.[47] Judge Dooling found after a year of research that the Pastoral Plan had been implemented. Dooling concluded that the anti-abortion movement was a creation of the Catholic Church. Though his decision was later overturned, this was done for reasons which did not invalidate his research or the conclusion he drew from it.

In like manner, the first three Presidents of the National Right to Life Committee, an antiabortion group created by the Catholic Church, were all Protestants: Marjory Mecklenburg, Mildred Jefferson, and Carolyn Gerster. Since 1980, however, Jack Willke, a Catholic, has been President.[48]

The U.S. Catholic bishops also do their lobbying through another organization, The National Committee For a Human Life Amendment. As Connie Paige has written in her book, "The Right To Lifers," the NCHLA, like the National Right To Life Committee, "was supposed to have no official connection with the Church. Its affiliation, however, was obvious from public records showing where it got the better part of its money, a good deal of it coming from Catholic communicants across the country. The link was also widely acknowledged within the right-to-life movement, where activists unhesitatingly referred to NCHLA as 'the bishops' outfit.' Yet another connection was through the person of the Reverend Edward Bryce, who was once head of NCHLA and now directs right-to-life activities for the National Conference of Catholic Bishops. The Reverend Bryce has presided over the transformation of the church into a right-to-life political machine."[49]

Jesse Helms, Protestant senior Senator from North Carolina, has served the Vatican well as "Dean of the New Right" in return for massive Catholic support—financial, organizational, and advisory in his 1978 and 1984 reelection campaigns. As I explore further in my book, *American Democracy and the Vatican*, "The biggest winner of all has been Senator Jesse Helms of North Carolina ... There is little doubt that Helms is the Vatican's most important ally in Congress and, precisely because he is non-Catholic, the most important of all to their agenda. No one has had greater access to the "hidden" money of the Catholic Church of which Father Bryce spoke. Helms is Baptist, but Congressional Club founder and Helms's campaign strategist since 1972, Thomas F. Ellis, is Catholic. Helms gained much of his fame for his ability to tie up the Senate with its own rules. However, it is his legislative aide, James P. Lucier, a Catholic, who "mastered the rules" and devised the strategies to accomplish this. The "Helms Amendment" barred use of U.S. Agency for International Development funds for assistance to programs providing abortions. It carried the name of a Protestant, but was written by Catholic John Sullivan."[50]

Another Catholic centrally involved is Paul Weyrich, a founder of Moral Majority, Christian Voice and Religious Roundtable. He openly claims credit for originating the idea for the Moral Majority and the name itself.[51] Weyrich's umbilical connection to Rome is manifest in his own words: "If we didn't know the Pope agrees with us, we Catholics in the New Right would have serious conscience problems. I would never work counter to the Church's official position."[52]

Richard A. Viguerie, a Catholic, devised the extraordinarily successful direct mail operations which resulted in membership claims of roughly four million Roman Catholics, Protestant fundamentalists, and orthodox Jews.[53] The organization claims its "hardcore contributors" number more than 400,000, including a cadre of 80,000 priests, ministers, and rabbis[54] organized into fifty chapters as detailed in the Bishops' Pastoral Plan of Action.

Putting the pastoral plan to work

Consistent with Part I of the Plan which calls for "a public information effort, directed to the general public," identification of the powerful Protestant electronic ministry with the goals of the Plan began to emerge in 1976 and 1977, shortly after the Plan was published. In order for the Bishops to cast abortion as a "religious and moral" issue (rather than just a Catholic issue) and communicate with the Protestant four-fifths of America, of course it has been useful to communicate through Protestant ministers. All of the politically oriented fundamentalist Protestant electronic ministers have risen to power since the initiation of the Pastoral Plan.[55] None had shown an interest in abortion previously and, in fact, fundamentalists, in general, had never objected to abortion until the Vatican actively cultivated the fundamentalists following publication of the Plan. Is it possible that the powerful electronic ministry owes its financial success to the wealthy Vatican and the Pastoral Plan? The Vatican certainly has every capability necessary for manipulating the electronic ministry.

Aiding and abetting the Pastoral Plan for Pro-Life Activities are Washington "think tanks" such as the Heritage Foundation, headed by Catholic Edwin Feulner and originally financed by Catholic Joseph Coors.[56] To assist its fund raising, the Foundation advertises that its publications are assiduously read by the White House. To defuse the security threats of overpopulation and illegal immigration, the Heritage Foundation has featured the economic growth theories of Julian Simon and the late Herman Kahn.

Other Washington "research" organizations producing intellectual and legal underpinnings for Reagan administration policies are the American Enterprise Institute, the Free Congress Foundation, the Washington Legal Foundation and the Center for Judicial Studies.[57] These organizations are serving as little more than Vatican lobbying organizations.

Recently, there have been increasing signs that the National Academy of Sciences (NAS) may have joined the ranks of these Vatican lobbying organizations as it prepares to put its prestige behind the Julian Simon mythology espoused by the Vatican.[58] In December 1983, the Vatican's Congregation for Catholic Education issued a document to all governments which included the following statement: "It is the task of the state to safeguard its citizens against injustice and moral disorders such as the . . . improper use of demographic information." (Ref. *American*

Democracy p.184) In other words, it is the responsibility of the governments to censor demographic information that suggests the existence of a population problem. If the forthcoming NAS report on population has indeed been "Simonized," is this another response of the Reagan administration to the Vatican's will?

Fortunately for the true conservative cause in the U.S., these groups and their adherents could not be considered as authentic American Conservatives in the image of Senators Barry Goldwater (R. Ariz.) and the late Sam J. Ervin, Jr. (D. N.C.). The "New Right" is not a conservative American political movement; it is mainly a religious one, directed by the American Catholic Bishops Conference and indirectly by the Vatican Curia. Rather than being American conservatives, these people are radicals who wish to make major changes in our constitution and changes in the long established relationships of our government institutions to each other.

During the four years 1980–1984, the Catholic Bishops' Pastoral Plan for Pro-Life Activities perfected its organizing plans for the 435 Congressional Districts to include the counties within them. So well did all the campaign elements function—such as the telephone networks, candidate files, secret societies such as the Knights of Malta and Opus Dei—and with ample financing of targeted candidates under the overall direction of Catholic Senator Paul Laxalt, Honorary Chairman of the Republican National Committee and President Reagan's Reelection Campaign, that the Republicans increased their percentage of the Catholic vote from 46% in 1980 to 58% in 1984.[59] This obviously had much to do with the 49 state victory of President Reagan.

The Pastoral Plan carefully targets the executive, legislative and judicial branches of our government. The emotional issue of abortion was used to justify the creation and implementation of this plan by the Vatican. Doesn't all this suggest that the Pastoral Plan is really a frank declaration of a holy war on American democracy?

Money and Catholic power

For more than 1,000 years, the Roman Catholic Church has shrouded its financial affairs in secrecy. Between 1975 and 1984 a number of voluntary and involuntary disclosures have thrown a little light on Vatican finances. David Yallop, in his best-selling book, *In God's Name: An Investigation into the Murder of Pope John Paul I*, (Bantam Books,

1984), submits substantial evidence that Pope John Paul I was killed by threatened insiders just as he prepared to vastly alter the birth control position and the financial organization of the Church.

The tragedy for the Roman Catholic Church and its communicants is that for the second time in a decade the opportunity to open the windows of the Vatican to the fresh air of a more liberal attitude on artificial birth control and other matters of great import to the world was thwarted and lost. With the elevation of Karol Wojtyla as Pope John Paul II, "business as usual" returned to the Vatican. None of the changes proposed by Pope John Paul I have been implemented. Vatican Incorporated is still functioning in all markets. World population continues to grow exponentially and the seepage of its excess across our borders increases alarmingly.

Yallop's book subjects Vatican finances to a detailed scrutiny, which I have attempted to summarize here. Yallop describes how Vatican productive wealth, quite apart from its priceless art collection and worldwide real estate holdings, rests largely on a portfolio built on a capital base of about $92 million. This fund, equivalent to $550 million in 1984, was a payment by Benito Mussolini to Pope Pius XI in 1929, as belated reparation for Vatican land taken over by the Italian state.

These assets are in the care of the Administration of the Patrimony of the Holy See (APSA). The head of the Prefecture for the Economic Affairs of the Holy See admitted to $125 million in assets in 1975, but no billions. According to Yallop, the Istitute per le Opere di Religione (IOR), the Vatican Bank, has been reported to have some $3 billion in assets, including 500,000 ounces of gold deposited with the Federal Reserve Bank of New York. These assets were built by a remarkable manager, Bernardino Nogara, between 1930 and 1958 by judicious investments in industrial and financial companies first in Italy and later in the United States and worldwide.

The annual profits of the Vatican Bank, estimated to be in excess of $100 million, are 85% available to the Pope. Parish priests forward a percentage of ordinary parish income to the diocese, but nothing compels a bishop to give from his coffers to Rome. So now, as in centuries past, an important source of papal revenue is Peter's Pence, an annual collection worldwide that goes to the Pope. Its amount is not revealed.

Wealthy archdioceses, such as Chicago in the United States and Munich in Germany, probably have bigger budgets than the Vatican. In the seventeen acrimonious years (1965–1982) during which Cardinal John

Cody ruled the Archdiocese of Chicago, it was revealed that the diocese had an annual revenue approaching $300 million. Although he made gifts to the Pope and members of the Curia, the Cardinal refused to release financial statements to anyone, including Rome or the IRS even when subpoenaed.

In 1968, Bishop Paul Marcinkus, a native of Cicero, Illinois, became manager of the Vatican Bank. He readily admitted "I have no banking experience." (Yallop, p. 121) To assist him in overcoming this deficiency, he obtained at Pope Paul VI's suggestion (p. 117) the help of two financial advisors—Michele Sindona, the president of banks in Milan, Messina, Geneva, Panama, and later the Franklin National Bank in New York; and in 1971 Roberto Calvi, President of the Banco Ambrosiano of Milan, Banco del Gottardo in Lugano, Switzerland, Banco Ambrosiano Overseas, Nassau, BWI, etc.

Yallop determined that one strategem of the Vatican Bank was to further diversify its remaining Italian holdings in order to "avoid heavy Italian taxation." (p. 124). To help accomplish this, Sindona added the lucrative practice of laundering the estimated $600 million annual heroin profit of the Sicilian Mafia Gambino family (p. 107). Roberto Calvi aided this by making available his Luxembourg company called Banco Ambrosiano Holdings and his offshore banks, and under the protection of the Vatican Bank laundered dollars back into Europe and Sicily from the United States and Canada. Other activities involved huge speculations in foreign exchange, rigging the Milan Stock Exchange, and embezzling funds from other depositors to finance these transactions.

It all ended with the 1974 collapse of the Franklin National Bank in New York with a loss to the Federal Deposit Insurance Corporation (U.S. taxpayers) of $2 billion, the biggest bank failure to that date in U.S. history. Sindona was arrested in New York, found guilty on sixty-five counts, and on June 13, 1980, sentenced to twenty-five years imprisonment and fined $200,000. Roberto Calvi was arrested by Milan authorities in May 1981, freed on bail under appeal, was found hanging under Blackfriars Bridge in the City of London on June 17, 1982. A few days later it was discovered that Banco Ambrosiano Milan was short $1.3 billion.

Bishop Marcinkus could justly claim to have done more than any other priest in modern times to bring the Roman Catholic Church into disrepute. Nevertheless, Pope John Paul II promoted him to Archbishop by making him Governor of Vatican City, where he remains in 1984, protected from the Italian authorities (p. 321). Roberto Calvi in early 1982 begged Marcinkus and the Pope to make good the $1.3 billion shortage of Banco Ambrosiano from the profits of their eleven-year partnership. At the time of this appeal, Calvi placed the patrimony of the Vatican Bank at $10 billion, instead of the $3 billion estimated above.

In the years before the Ambrosiano failure, a number of international banks (including U.S.) had loaned Calvi's Luxembourg holding company $600 million. Afterward, the Vatican began wrangling with the Italian government and a consortium representing these international banks regarding the $600 million indebtedness. Agreement was finally reached by mid-May 1984. As reported by the financial press, the international banks will get back approximately two-thirds, or $400 million of their loans. Of this sum, the Vatican Bank will pay $240 million, "on the basis of non-culpability but in recognition of a moral involvement."

As a result of these glimpses into the wealth of the Vatican and its dioceses, it is evident that the Church enjoys vast economic power. In a democracy, political power can be acquired by buying elections. Running for office has become very expensive indeed. The Vatican has taken full advantage of this development, reaching into its large treasure to influence office seekers in the United States, thus helping to implement its 1975 Pastoral Plan for Pro-Life Activities.

However the most important lesson to be learned from Yallop's book is that the Vatican is a demonstrably corrupt institution that has widely abused its power. Furthermore, Yallop, with considerable evidence in hand, concluded that the Vatican killed its own pope in order to protect its power. (This is explored further in Appendix 4.) Therefore, it is not unreasonable to assume that the Vatican would undermine American democracy, through widespread corruption, to protect its power.

The Engineering of Subversion

The Reagan administration has been the most Catholic in American history. It is increasingly obvious to many observers other than myself that its policies, and attempts to overturn long-standing programs, and even constitutional principles, resonate with the Vatican agenda.

Consider these parallels: Both are anti-abortion, anti-Equal Rights Amendment, pro-school prayer, anti-domestic family planning, anti-international population assistance, pro-tuition tax credits, anti-environment, anti-sex education, anti-United Nations, pro-illegal immigration (especially for Catholics), anti-federal aid to public education, anti-gay rights, anti-separation of church and state, and both are anti-communist. (A more complete list of examples and a discussion of each can be found in Chapter 10 of *American Democracy*.[37])

The leadership of the Roman Catholic Church in America is largely Irish. Most U.S. Cardinals and Bishops are Irish.[60] Can this be related to the fact that most of the key positions in the Reagan administration are occupied by Irish Catholics?

With 52 million claimed communicants, Roman Catholics constitute 22.5% of the U.S. population of 236 million. About 4 percent of the

U.S. population is Irish Roman Catholic.[60] President Ronald Reagan's father, like the leadership of the Catholic Church in America, was an Irish Catholic, and his brother is a devout Catholic. No one doubts the president's close ties to the Catholic Church. His empathy with Pope John Paul II is understandable as a result of the survival by both men of assassination attempts.

The Reagan administration: most Catholic in U.S. history

In any administration, the appointments most relevant to the population growth-national security issue are: National Security Advisor, Secretary of State (AID), Director of the Central Intelligence Agency (CIA), Attorney-General (responsible for the Immigration and Naturalization Service [INS] and the Border Patrol) and Secretary of Health and Human Services (HHS) (who sets the national example for provision of comprehensive family planning services).

Mr. Reagan has appointed three National Security Advisors: Richard Allen, William Clark and Robert McFarlane. Allen and Clark are Irish Catholics. His two Secretaries of State have been Alexander Haig, an Irish Catholic, and George Schultz, a Catholic of German extraction. His CIA Director is William Casey, an Irish Catholic, as is his Attorney-General, William French Smith, and his HHS Secretary Margaret Heckler.

During Mr. Reagan's first term in office, the three key people in the White House deciding whom he would see were James Baker, Michael Deaver and Edwin Meese. They are all Protestants. They have been replaced by former Secretary of the Treasury, Donald Regan, an Irish Catholic. Early in 1985, Irish Catholic Patrick Buchanan was appointed to the important post of Press Secretary. Joining still another Irish Catholic in the Cabinet, Secretary of Labor Raymond Donovan, are two more Irish Catholics, Vernon Walters, Ambassador to the United Nations, and William Bennett, Secretary of Education.

In a nation in which 22% of the population is Roman Catholic, and only 4 percent of the population is Irish Catholic, this causes no small concern. The odds of this arrangement happening by chance are nil. Now that it has become apparent that the agenda of the Reagan administration and the Vatican are harmonious, concern on the part of those who understand the security threat has turned into alarm.

Because the future of the political Catholic Church in the U.S. is imminently threatened by the solutions to the overpopulation problem, the Vatican has been driven to act with boldness. The creation, publication and implementation of the 1975 National Conference of Catholic Bishops' *Pastoral Plan for Pro-Life Activities* is a good indication of the Church's desperate attempts to reverse the population growth control movement.

A striking example of this occurred during the markup of the Simpson/Mazzoli Immigration Reform Bill (H.R. 1510) on May 4, 1985 by the House Judiciary Committee, with Chairman Peter W. Rodino, Jr., of New Jersey, presiding. Under consideration was the Moorhead Amendment which set a 450,000 annual ceiling on the number of legal immigrants, including immediate family relatives and preference system admissions, but no refugee admissions. The reason for the amendment was that the United States has no ceiling on legal immigration. There had been general agreement between proponents of reform and the Chairman that the U.S. should restore a ceiling on the number of immigrants legally entering our country each year.

When the roll call vote occurred, Chairman Rodino (a Catholic) pulled nine proxies from his pocket which added to his own vote and nine Democrat votes present made 19 against 11 Republican votes for the ceiling. The vote was a startling surprise to most observers. The next day it was learned that about five days previously a delegation of five Bishops from the National Council of Catholic Bishops had called on Chairman Rodino at his Washington office to urge that there be no ceiling on legal immigration into the United States.

Social engineering weapons

The charge of *anti-Catholicism* has been a handy social engineering weapon used by the Vatican for a long time, especially in the U.S. Religious tolerance is strongly woven into the fabric of American society. One does not criticize another's religion. The charge of anti-Catholicism tends to have what lawyers call a "chilling effect" on anyone wanting to criticize the Catholic Church on any account. Those few who do overcome this fear of being labeled "anti-Catholic" are often ostracized. Yet like anyone else, Catholics, including the Pope, are not infallible. However, to accept the automatic charge of anti-Catholism is to say that Catholics are above criticism. Recently, Jack Willke, President of the National Right to Life Committee (NRLC), stated that Americans who favor legalized family planning or legalized abortion are anti-Catholic. It appears that by his definition, anyone who threatens the political power of the Vatican in any way, is anti-Catholic. Hence, Americans who favor birth control are anti-Catholic.

The powerful social taboo placed on thinking in terms of a "conspiracy" is another important social engineering weapon used by the Vatican. This too has been woven into the American social fabric, and is now used against anyone who might claim that the Vatican has political ambitions in America.

An example of this taboo is that in the 120 years since President Lincoln was assassinated, there has been only silence about the fact that Booth and 4 conspirators hung by our government for their roles in his assassination were all Catholics, all having been aided by many priests. Ex-Priest Emmett McLoughlin documents this conspiracy in his book, *An Inquiry into the Assassination of President Lincoln* (Lyle Stuart, Inc., 1963). Some of his findings are provided in Appendix 5.

Is the Bishops' 1975 *Pastoral Plan for Pro-life Activities* a blueprint for a Vatican conspiracy to undermine American democracy? This taboo deters public discussion of the Plan in the light of such a blunt question. *The National Catholic Reporter* once said the Plan will lead to a Catholic political party in America,[61] such as, the Christian Democratic parties in Europe and El Salvador. Given the inordinate amount of influence exercised by the Vatican in both the Democratic party and now the Republican party, however, both parties may have been co-opted.

Putting Vatican interests on top

Nowhere is it clearer that the best interests of the Vatican have superseded those of the U.S. than in matters concerning the population growth-national security issue.

In May 1984, the White House began circulating its policy statement prepared for the World Population Conference in Mexico City,[62] as I touched on earlier. Its echoing of Vatican views on family planning, abortion and population growth control was immediately evident. During the Conference, the U.S. delegation, which was decidedly Catholic in orientation and headed by Irish Catholics James Buckley and James Malone, stood with the Vatican in opposition to the positions taken by virtually all of the other 150 countries present. The government delegates of these 150 countries noted that the Vatican and the U.S. delegation acted as one, much to the embarrassment of many American observers present.

According to the Reagan administration policy statement, as I've also noted, the world population crisis has been caused not by too many people but by too much government planning, bad economic policies and "anti-intellectualism," basically a Vatican-ordained position. "The combinations of these two factors—counterproductive economic policies in poor and struggling nations, and a pessimism among the more advanced—led to a demographic overreaction in the 1960s and 1970s," the U.S. Statement said. "Scientific forecasts were required to compete with unsound, extremist scenarios, and too many governments pursued population control measures without sound economic policies that create the rise in living standards historically associated with decline in fertility rates."

To the Administration policy statement, Robert S. McNamara, former World Bank president, responded, "I think we Americans will be laughed out of the conference if they stress that theme. It's absurd."[63] For some reason, one vital element is always left out of Reagan Administration and Vatican policy statements on population growth. Sharp reductions in growth rates do not *automatically* occur with economic development. Only increasing use of modern methods of family planning and widespread use of abortion (generally 500 or more abortions per 1000 live births as we have in the U.S.) results in significant reductions in growth rates,[45] yet both the Vatican and the Reagan administration are working very hard to eliminate or curb support of fertility control assistance irrespective of "economic policies."

Immigration tidal wave

Probably, the most immediate threat to U.S. security in this global context is the legal and illegal immigration (an estimated 2 million people immigrated into this country in 1984) primarily from Latin America but also from Asia and the Middle East. The Census Bureau has not released any numbers or estimates. Private organizations have advanced a low, conservative figure of 12 to 20 million illegal immigrants in the United States at the end of 1984. Several years ago, the Gallup International Research Institute conducted the first world-wide public opinion poll.[64] This survey found that more than one out of every four Latin Americans wanted to permanently emigrate to the U.S., a proportion that has most certainly increased by now. If they were able to do so and given the high fertility rate of the 400 million people of Latin America, then within 20 years, the U.S. population could approximately double to 470 million. Meanwhile, the Vatican is seeking to block every substantial effort to check illegal immigration. Not surprisingly, an estimated 90 percent of illegal aliens currently in the U.S. are Catholics.

Why is the Vatican pressing on the United States a population policy on immigration which is clearly not in our national self-interest? A doubling of the U.S. population with Latin American Catholics would mean, in due course, a U.S. population that is 60 percent Catholic. The worldwide political power of the Vatican would be enormously enhanced with a Latin style "democracy" in America. The longer the Vatican can maintain the current U.S. "open borders" position, the more enhanced its power will become.

Evidence from numerous sources supports the contention that the Roman Catholic Church is the leading smuggler of illegal aliens across the southern border of the U.S. from Latin American Countries—using church properties and vehicles to provide "sanctuary."[65,66,67,68] A number of Protestant denominations, not to be outdone in "compassion," have copied these sanctuary procedures and receive virtually all of the press. Private Mafia type smuggling rings are reported to charge $500 to $1500 for each alien, depending on terminal cities. The smuggling of aliens is a felony in the United States. By the end of 1984, the Department of Justice had ordered no arrests of church smugglers.

We all are compassionate, surely, toward people whose countries have become so overpopulated that 50% unemployment, social instability and warfare are rampant. Nonetheless, the U.S. cannot begin to accommodate even a fraction of those seeking jobs within its borders. As many as nine out of ten of today's illegal immigrants are seeking jobs here, most of which are also being sought by American unemployed.

A careful distinction must be made between economic and political refugees; if the definition is so broad as to include the former, over half the world's population will qualify as refugees. If everyone is a refugee, no one is. Determination of whether an illegal alien is a political refugee deserving asylum or an economic job seeker is the responsibility of the state, or of the United Nations High Commissioner for Refugees, not of an ecclesiastical body, priests or ministers. "Render unto Caesar the things which are Caesar's." In America, it is our birthright to have a government of laws and not of men.

Late in 1984, with White House support, we almost witnessed passage of the Vatican-supported, much modified and gutted, Simpson/Mazzoli immigration bill that would have insured "open borders" for many years to come. A law that does not contain provisions for a non-forgeable social security card, employer sanctions, a very conservative or no amnesty provision, and a vastly expanded Immigration and Naturalization Service (particularly the Border Patrol), is doomed to certain failure. Despite the seriousness of the political and economic threat of illegal immigration to U.S. national security, no substantial preparations are evident within our government to counter this threat. This is another example of how Vatican interests are being placed ahead of U.S. interests in the realm of population policy, primarily by Catholics who owe their loyalty to the Vatican (the political Church) rather than America.

The growth of Catholic dissent

Many Americans, including Catholics, agree with another Irish Catholic American, former CIA Director William Colby, who has stated that "world population growth is the greatest threat to U.S. security."[69] Greater than thermonuclear war. Of great importance is the fact that, like Colby, most Catholic Americans do not subscribe to the Vatican position on fertility control. About 88% of both Catholic and nonCatholic U.S. women exposed to the risk of unintended pregnancy are currently using contraception.[70] Catholic Americans use the same contraceptive methods[71] and have the same positive attitudes toward abortion as non-Catholic Americans,[72] and they have the same desired family sizes.[73] Furthermore, most American Catholics disagree with the Vatican on the need for population growth control.

Certainly there are devout Catholics, who out of ingrained obedience or deep religious conviction, follow Vatican doctrine on these issues. It is to be expected also, since Catholics share human frailties with the rest of us, that there is another stratum of less devout Catholic clergy and laity who go along with present doctrine and receive rewards ranging from approval to career advancement, "for good behavior." And it is natural that a great many Catholics who disagree with present doctrine and disobey it, do not want to take issue with Catholicism and the emotional satisfactions the Church has given them and their families; indeed this group quite probably constitutes a strong 'silent majority.' Meanwhile, nonetheless, open vocal dissent by Catholics has grown loud and clear on the issues of contraception, abortion and population. Yet so far, apparently, this has served only to make the present Pope and the Curia more intransigent.

Infringing on U.S. Sovereignty

Vatican infringements, or attempted intrusions, on national sovereignty are not a new phenomenon. In 1962, Pope John XXIII told columnist Robert Blair Kaiser of the Vatican's holy war against communist governments, which the Church felt must be overthrown.[74] For 80 years the French protected the Catholic minority government in Vietnam (only 5 percent of the country was Catholic) from the Buddhist majority. When the French recognized the popularity of the Buddhist uprising and the futility of their efforts, they pulled out. Was America called upon by the Vatican to fill the vacuum?

Spellman: the Papal hawk on Vietnam

Among the many examples of Vatican infringement on American sovereignty offered by John Cooney in his best-selling book, *The American Pope: The Life and Times of Francis Cardinal Spellman* (Times Books, 1984), is Vietnam. Cooney concluded that the Vietnam war became an "American" cause in large measure because of Spellman's public and private lobbying. Even before the French defeat at

Dienbienphu, the U.S. had underwritten 80% of the French war costs. Spellman, for months before the defeat, had tried unsuccessfully to pressure the administration into beefing up assistance to the French troops. "The Cardinal declared that Vietnam was vital to the preservation of . . . Catholicism."[75]

Spellman's Vietnam stance was in accordance with the wishes of Pope Pius XII. Malachi Martin, a former Jesuit priest who worked in the Vatican during the years of the escalating U.S. commitment to Vietnam, said the Pope wanted the U.S. to back Diem. "The Pope was concerned about Communism making more gains at the expense of the Church," said Martin, "and he turned to Spellman to encourage American commitment to Vietnam."[76]

Spellman discovered Diem in 1950 while the latter, a lay celibate and deeply religious Catholic, was a student at the Catholic Maryknoll Seminary in Ossining, New York. According to Cooney, "In Diem, Spellman had seen the qualities he desired in any leader: ardent Catholicism and rabid anti-Communism."[77] More than anyone else, Spellman nurtured Diem's rise to power and with Joseph Kennedy formed a pro-Diem lobby in Washington. The rallying cries of the lobby were Catholicism and anti-Communism and the leadership was mostly Catholic, including co-chairmen Generals "Wild Bill" Donovan and "Iron Mike" O'Daniel, Senator John Kennedy and Monsignor Harnett.[78] Says Cooney, "By 1963, Spellman became one of the most hawkish, arguably the most hawkish, leaders in the United States."[79]

The Vatican influence in that war remained until the waning moments, as highlighted by U.S. Ambassador Graham Martin's sharp response to criticism of his policy of holding back Americans in the evacuation of the Saigon Embassy compound, while putting Catholic Vietnamese aboard the helicopters. "Among Americans here is Father McVeigh, head of the Catholic Relief Service, who will not leave without his Vietnamese staff . . . How will the President [Richard Nixon] explain to . . . Cardinal Cooke, Father McVeigh's great and good friend, why I left him?"[80] The Vatican's "holy war" to save the only Catholic government on the Asian mainland from Communism cost 58,000 American and 2,000,000 Vietnamese lives.

Running U.S. foreign policy from Rome

More recently, in the "holy war" in Lebanon, in an attempt to save the Catholic minority government there, 241 American marines died despite the futility of the situation and the urgent advice from military strate-gists to withdraw. In a newsbrief commemorating the first anniversary of this terrorist attack, a CBS correspondent said, "The only purpose of the presence of the marines was to protect the minority Catholic government."

Another example is much closer to home. President Reagan, in a speech in Hoboken, New Jersey, on July 26, 1984, declared that he was following the leadership of Pope John Paul II in determining U.S. for-eign policy in Central America.[81] This is the latest effort to save Vatican-backed governments of overpopulated countries from popular uprisings. The Vatican wishes to maintain the status quo in Latin America, since its political power in the region is currently maximized. This is the Vatican agenda, but when our President adopts it, what does this say to us about the separation of church and state?

Secret legions

The Vatican acts in part, often soundlessly and most effectively, through a relatively small number of Americans who give the Church their loyalty for reasons unrelated to religious practice, but rather for advancement, power and privilege. This is accomplished with great skill and subtlety through secret organizations such as Opus Dei and the Knights of Malta.

According to Father Andrew Greeley, "Opus Dei is a devious, anti-democratic, reactionary, semi-fascist institution, desperately hungry for absolute power in the Church and quite possibly very close now to having that power. Calling the group "authoritarian and power-mad," the American Catholic priest and author said, "Opus Dei is an extremely dangerous organization because it appeals to the love of secrecy and the power lust of certain kinds of religious personalities. It may well be the most powerful group in the Church today. It is capable of doing an enormous amount of harm. It ought to be forced to come out into the open or be suppressed."

In a recent *Church & State*, Religious News Service's Rome cor-respondent Eleni Dimmler estimates that worldwide there are 74,000 in the most devoted membership categories (1300 are priests) and 700,000 Opus Dei "cooperators." "With this international 'army' of devoted members, Opus Dei has created an impressive network of activities in countries around the world . . . According to a 1979 memo, members of the movement work, among other things, at

487 universities and schools, 694 newspapers and periodicals, 52 TV or radio stations, 38 publicity agencies and twelve film companies."[82]

The March 19, 1984, issue of *U.S. News and World Report* examined these two secret Catholic elite religious societies:[83] the Knights of Malta with one thousand U.S. members who are prominent in government, business, or professional life and Opus Dei with three thousand U.S. members of widely varied backgrounds. The number of U.S. members in the "cooperator" category has not been revealed but could amount to more than 100,000.

The central tenet of Opus Dei is to "help shape the world in a Catholic manner" and its American members include "priests, middle and upper-class businessmen, professionals, military personnel and government officials."[84]

The Knights of Malta dates back to the time of the Crusades; its present members are reported to include some of our nation's most prominent Catholics: CIA Director William Casey; William Wilson; Vernon Walters; Senators Denton and Domenici; Alexander Haig; William Sloan; and William F. Buckley, creator and leader of Young Americans for Freedom, from which many of the Reagan administration team have been drawn. According to members, the order serves "as an international defender of the Church."[83]

In June of each year a ceremony is held in Rome for Knights of Malta which includes the "swearing of allegiance to the defense of the Holy Mother Church."[84] Herein lies the problem for population growth control and its recognition as a national security issue. The Knights are committed to defending the Church. Only the most devout and obedient are invited to join the Knights and Opus Dei (which its detractors have compared to mind-controlling cults).[84] If the Vatican has determined that population growth control threatens the Holy Mother Church, the members of these societies are obliged to counter this threat by thwarting the development of population growth control government policies and their execution.

The Vatican vs. humanity

So it was inevitable, it seems to me, that the interests of the Vatican and those of the United States would clash on the issue of curbing population growth. No one can swear and abide by complete allegiance to both the United States and the Roman Catholic Church. The reported acts and attitudes of the Knights of Malta in the Reagan Administration seem to reflect complete allegiance to the Pope rather than our country. If these reports are true, should the members of these societies be considered traitors to our country?

As long as this conflict of allegiance exists in our midst, the U.S. cannot act with the leadership it exercised until recently to assist other nations in curbing population growth. The real problem is not convincing people that they must have small families, or delivering family planning services to them. This we could most certainly achieve by the end of the century for most of the world's people at a price we can well afford. The profound problem right now is the conflict between the priorities of the Pope and his Church and his hierarchy and the desperate need of humanity to control its fertility.

All American Catholics are certain to pay a high price for this intrusion of their Church leaders into American sovereignty. In 1969, the so-called Soccer War was fought between El Salvador and Honduras. This was the first war ever directly attributed to overpopulation, a determination made by the Organization of American States.[85] The war was prompted by massive illegal immigration from grossly overpopulated El Salvador into Honduras. Fifteen years later, the overpopulation problem continues to be all but ignored in El Salvador. The population in 1984 is growing at the rate of 2.6 percent per year, giving the country a doubling time of 27 years![86] The results of this continued growth have been the illegal immigration of more than 500,000 Salvadorans to the United States (1 in 9 of that country's native population),[87] a breakdown in social order and destruction of the economic, social and political structures of the country.

This climate of turmoil is bound to invade the U.S. itself, I'm convinced, if we allow continued illegal immigration of tens of millions of Latin Americans and others into our country. This approach to assuming control over the once most powerful nation on earth appears to be what the Vatican has in mind. Meanwhile, the Catholic hierarchy remains by far the most significant opposition to illegal immigration control.

Reclaiming Our Options

El Salvador and China illustrate the narrow choice of American options if we continue to allow a power other than our own democratically representative government to dictate U.S. foreign and domestic policy on family planning and population growth control activities. We are threatened with becoming either an insecure nation in social, economic and political chaos, such as El Salvador except on a huge scale, or becoming a highly regimented nation like China, devoid of many of our cherished freedoms. Neither option is acceptable. Population growth control is the only alternative.

The "holy war" against population growth control and American democracy is no longer a covert operation in America. It was launched by a small number of Catholics who serve the Vatican interests, and is now aided by non-Catholics who have been co-opted by them. Only our silence in the face of the Vatican's energy, organization and direction of the anti-abortion, anti-family-planning, anti-population-growth-control movement in the U.S. makes continuation of this war possible. Now that they perceive what's been happening, more Americans are beginning to speak out against this increasingly open Catholic strategy. More of us, great and small, must do so.

The inevitable American confrontation with the Vatican on the issue of population growth control has already begun. In due time, those who have chosen to place the interests of another sovereignty before U.S. national interests must weigh their position against the judgments of their countrymen. How destructive this confrontation will be to America and Americans, both Catholic and non-Catholics, depends on how long it is postponed.

It is a pity, and could be painfully destructive of our American social and political fabric, but public trust in American Catholics generally is threatened by the Vatican's invasion of American sovereignty, and its interference in our internal affairs. If American non-Catholics sense a breach of national faith by a significant number of Catholics who appear to be more loyal to the Vatican than to their country, public trust in Catholics generally, and especially those in public office, will be destroyed. If the Vatican proceeds, a violent reaction is already predictable.

The year 1984 did not prove to be as Orwellian as the English author had prophesied. But a threat in some ways similar had emerged in America quite clearly. It was a Presidential election year for us, and also the year that President Reagan restored full diplomatic relations with the Holy See by appointing the first U.S. Ambassador to the Vatican in more than a century, and receiving the Vatican's Papal Nuncio in Washington. On September 12th, as the Presidential campaign revved up for its final weeks, commentator Bill Moyers appeared on the CBS Evening News with Dan Rather. Moyers noted that "politicians almost always go hunting for votes in the precincts of the faithful." And he asked, "So what's new in this campaign?"

Moyers continued, "This is new: Conservative Catholics and Protestants have openly allied themselves with the Republican Party in a way that threatens to turn the public debate on morality into a partisan crusade and make Mr. Reagan's party the party of religion. That would be a profound change in American politics . . . In time, nothing but trouble is likely to come of a major political party's commitment to the doctrinal triumph of a sectarian notion of God's will for America."

Moyers concluded, "We have in this country an admirable alternative to civil war, and to holy civil war at that. It's called the Constitution."[88]

"The Time Has Come"

To be sure, the Constitution is our ultimate guardian of the separation of church and state. But it will be a sad and tragic day if Constitutional redress alone is all that saves us from the clear and present dangers explored in this book. The people themselves can speak out and act on these dangers now, in all the ways that are part of our cherished democratic process, which indeed the Constitution also protects. The essence of the danger is embedded quite pithily in the comments of a senior Jesuit priest, quoted two years ago in *The New York Times Magazine*. He spoke the truth which he then immediately denied:

> "The idea that human society must be entirely subordinated to the purposes of the Church—we have gotten away from this. The layman was emancipated by Vatican II from this terrible kind of clericalism and authority."[89]

The fact is the Church has indeed sought to subordinate human society as a whole—not just Catholics—"to the purposes of the Church." The fact is it still does, as the recent Extraordinary Synod of Bishops in Rome so clearly revealed, despite the polite circumlocutions the bishops expressed at its conclusion. The Vatican "holy war" against family planning is the example *par excellence* of present Church efforts to subordinate human society to its own agenda, subverting our Constitutional rights as it implacably proceeds.

Placing the interest of the Church ahead of the interest of humanity is not religion. It is done in the name of religion but it is done for reasons of power, pure and simple. Placing the needs of an institution, any institution, including the Papacy, ahead of the needs of humanity, is anti-humanistic by definition.

Since the Vatican seeks to subordinate the rights and public policy preferences of all Americans, including Protestants and Jews, to the purposes of its holy war on family planning, this governing principle of the Church is obviously anti-American as well. We have every right, indeed obligation, to be angered by and to object to this holy war that has been declared against us. This book calls into question the belief that a democratic America and the Vatican can coexist.

A Note to the Reader

If you are alarmed by the evidence Dr. Mumford presents about the threats to family planning and population growth control efforts, and to the constitutional foundations of American democracy, you can help by spreading the word about these threats. Please consider sending a copy of this book to friends, colleagues, ministers, local editors, teachers, professors, national, state and local officials. Additional copies at substantial discounts may be obtained by writing The Center for Research on Population and Security, P.O. Box 13067, Research Triangle Park, North Carolina 27709.

For further documentation and a more complete discussion of the issue sketched in this book, including the more than 400 sources Dr. Mumford used to reach his conclusions, see: American Democracy and the Vatican: Population Growth and National Security, by Stephen D. Mumford published by Humanist Press, 7 Harwood Drive, Amherst, New York 14226-0146, 1985. ($7.95 paperback, $11.95 hardcover)

References

1. Jim Fain, Cox News Service, *San Francisco Chronicle*, August 21, 1985.
2. Eleanor Smeal, special by Phil Gailey to the *New York Times*, September 6, 1985.
3. *Options*, Religious Coalition for Abortion Rights Education Fund, Inc. Summer 1985.
4. "Mexico, O Mexico!" James Reston, *New York Times*, September 29, 1985.
5. *Syracuse Herald-Register*, March 23, 1985.
6. G.H.L. Zeegers, "The Meaning of the Population Problem of the World," *Cross Currents*, Winter 1958, p.19.
7. *Church and State*, October 1985.
8. Ibid.
9. "The Righteous Fanatics," Anthony Lewis, *New York Times*, September 28, 1984.
10. *New York Times*, November 11, 1985.
11. Lester R. Brown, "Stopping Population Growth," *State of the World 1985*, p.201.
12. Lester R. Brown, op cit, p.202.
13. *Newsweek*, June 25, 1984.
14. "The Population Problem," Robert S. McNamara, *Foreign Affairs*, Summer 1984.
15. Catholics for a Free Choice, statement in the *New York Times*, October 7, 1984.
16. *New York Times*, August 25, 1985.
17. Ibid.
18. *New York Times*, August 14, 1985.
19. Ibid.

20. John Kenneth Galbraith, "Reagan's Facts'—Artistic License." *New York Times,* September 27, 1985.

21. *The Time Has Come,* John Rock, M. D., Alfred A. Knopf, New York, 1963.

22. Ibid.

23. Senator Sam J. Ervin, on the television program "Work and Fulfillment." PBS stations, January 1980.

24. Op cit.

25. Conner R, Special Washington Report, Federation for American Immigration Reform (FAIR), Washington, D.C. October 11, 1984. p.2.

26. "Gallup Poll Confirms Increasing Numbers of Americans Want Immigration Reform." *FAIR/Immigration Report* 4(3):2, 1983.

27. "Public Opinion on Immigration." *Federation for American Immigration Reform,* Washington DC. 1984.

28. Greeley, AM. *The Making of the Popes 1978: The politics of Intrigue in the Vatican.* Kansas City: Andrews and McMeel, Inc., 1979.

29. Vaillancourt, JG. *Papal Power: A Study of Vatican Control Over Lay Catholic Elites.* Berkeley: University of California Press, 1980.

30. Greeley. p.37.

31. U.S. International Population Policy, Third Annual Report of the National Security Council Ad Hoc Group on Population Policy, January, 1979, Department of State.

32. U.S. International Population Policy, Fourth Annual Report of the National Security Council Ad Hoc Group on Population Policy, April, 1980, Department of State.

33. "Apprehensions Top 1.3 Million in 1985." Federation for American Immigration Reform. *FAIR/Immigration Report* 6(2):1, 1985.

34. "Why Immigration Reform?" *TEF DATA:* The Environmental Fund, Washington,D.C. No. 19, August 1985. p.1.

35. Testimony of Ambassador Marshall Green, Coordinator of Population Affairs, Department of State, before the Select Committee on Population, U.S. House of Representatives, February 7, 1978.

36. *Overpopulation Primer.* The Environmental Fund, Washington D.C. 1984.

37. Mumford, SD. *American Democracy & The Vatican: Population Growth & National Security.* Amherst, New York: Humanist Press, 1984. p.23.

38. Vining D.R.,Jr. Airborne Migrant Study Urged. Population Reference Bureau, Washington D.C. *INTERCOM* 7(11):3, 1979.

39. "Non-Mexican Apprehensions Increase." *FAIR/Immigration Report* 5(10):3, 1985.

40. Jones A. Vatican, "International Agencies Hone Family, Population Positions." *National Catholic Reporter* (reprinted in *Conscience,* May/June 1984, p.7).

41. "The Words of a Future Pope." *Los Angeles Times,* October 18, 1978. p.7.

42. Yallop, DA. *In God's Name: An Investigation into the Murder of Pope John Paul I.* New York: Bantam Books, 1984. p.24.

43. Jones. p.9.

44. Ibid. p.28.

45. Mumford, SD and Kessel, E. *Is Wide Availability of Abortion Essential to National Population Growth Control Programs? Experiences of 116 Countries.* American Journal of Obstetrics and Gynecology 149(6):639, 1984.

46. Paige,C. *The Right to Lifers: Who They Are, How They Operate, Where They Get*

Their Money. New York: Summit Books, 1983. p.155.

47. Federal Judge John Dooling's 1980 U.S. District Court, Eastern District of New York, decision in McRae vs. HEW.

48. Ibid. pp.83—87.

49. Ibid. p.63.

50. *American Democracy and The Vatican.* p.209.

51. Young, P.D. Richard A. Viguerie: The New Right's Secret Power Broker. *Penthouse,* December 1982. p.146.

52. Negri, M. "The Well-Planned Conspiracy." *The Humanist* 42(3):40, 1982.

53. *U.S. News and World Report.* June 21, 1982.

54. Ibid.

55. Winston D. Three articles. 1. "TV Preachers' Message: For God and Country" (p.1A). 2. "Televangelists Bring Change to Religious Programming" (p.17A). 3. "Religious Labels Sometimes Difficult to Pin on TV Preachers" (p.16A). *Raleigh News and Observer.* February 17, 1985.

56. Young, P.D. *God's Bullies.* New York: Holt, Rinehart and Winston, 1982. p.127.

57. "Theorists on Right Find Fertile Ground." *Washington Post.* August 9, 1985.

58. Harrington W. "The Heretic Becomes Respectable." *Washington Post Magazine,* August 18, 1985. p.8.

59. "Reagan-Bush wins voter support-Catholic Vote-58% from 46% in 1980 (largest percentage increase in a voter group from the last election)." *First Monday,* National Republican Committee, March, 1985.

60. Ginder, R. *Binding with Briars: Sex and Sin in the Catholic Church.* Englewood Cliffs: Prentice-Hall, 1975. p.17.

61. "U.S. Bishops Spark New Abortion Debate." *INTERCOM* 4(1):13, 1976.

62. *American Democracy & The Vatican.* See Appendix 3.

63. "More funding urged for world population programs," *Raleigh News and Observer,* August 8, 1984. p.3A.

64. "The Environmental Fund Testifies Before the House and Senate Subcommittees Considering the Immigration Reform Act." *The Other Side* No. 31, p.2. March/April 1983.

65. Doan M. "Sanctuary: Churches' Way to Protest." *U.S. News & World Report,* September 24, 1984. p.45.

66. Murphy C. "Sanctuary: Churches Aiding Illegal Aliens." *Washington Post.* September 4, 1984. p.A1.

67. Taylor Jr. S. "16 Indicted by U.S. in Bid to End Church Smuggling of Latin Aliens." *New York Times,* January 15, 1985. p.A1.

68. Bole W. "Sanctuary." *Church & State,* 36(3):15,1983.

69. "Population." *Cincinnati Enquirer,* August 13, 1978.

70. Bachrach, CA." Contraceptive Practice Among American Women, 1973—1982." *Family Planning Perspectives* 19(6):253,1984.

71. Ibid.

72. Smith, TW. "Catholic Attitudes Toward Abortion." *Conscience* 5(4):6, 1984.

73. "Traditional Large Family of American Catholics Is No Longer The Norm." *Family Planning Perspectives* 10(4):241, 1978. From Westoff, CF. and Jones, EF. The End of "Catholic" Fertility (paper presented at the annual meeting of the Population

Association of America, Atlanta, 12–15 April 1978).

74. Kaiser, RB. "Unholy Wars in the Name of God." *U.S.A. Today,* August 23, 1984, p.4A.
75. Cooney, J. *The American Pope: The Life and Times of Francis Cardinal Spellman.* New York: Times Books, 1984. p.239.
76. Cooney. p.242.
77. Ibid. p.240.
78. Ibid. p.242.
79. Ibid. p.245.
80. Strasser, S., Kasindorf, M., Manning, R., Smith, VE. "55 Days of Shame." *Newsweek,* April 15, 1985. p.46.
81. Clines FX. "Reagan Courts Ethnic Voters by Assailing Foes." *New York Times,* July 27, 1985. p.A10.
82. Dimmler E. "Opus Dei: John Paul's Holy Mafia." *Church & State* 38(8):13, 1985.
83. Mann J. and Phillips K. "Inside Look at Those Elite Religious Groups." *U.S. News and World Report,* March 19, 1984. p.60.
84. Lee MA. "Their Will Be Done." *Mother Jones,* July 1983. p.22.
85. "Understanding El Salvador." *FAIR/Immigration Report* 4(6):2, 1984.
86. Kent, MM. and Haub C. 1984 World Population Data Sheet of the Population Reference Bureau, Inc. Washington DC, 1984.
87. Connor, R. Federation for American Immigration Reform. *FAIR/Immigration Report* 5(5):1, February 1985.
88. Transcript from CBS Evening News. September 12, 1984.
89. Kamm H. "The Secret World of Opus Dei." *New York Times Magazine,* January 1, 1984. p.85.

Appendices

APPENDIX

Appendix 1
Rev. John H. Galbreath on the
Presbyterian Position on Abortion

Testimony of the Rev. John H. Galbreath before the Presbyterian Church (USA) General Assembly Committee on Justice and Human Rights, May 31, 1984

I am grateful for the privilege to appear before you. My credentials arise from 35 years of experience as a pastor and as preacher of the Word. I know of no issue on which I speak with more commitment than that which is before us. Others speak more capably than I on the sociological, psychological and legal aspects of the right to terminate pregnancy. I make my case on the Biblical and theological issues involved and upon my deep commitment to personal freedom as currently guaranteed by the constitution of the United States of America.

At the heart of the abortion issue is the question of the full humanity of the fetus. The determination as to when one becomes a "person" is essentially theological in nature. The word "abortion" does not appear in Scripture. However, the experience is referred to on two occasions. In Exodus 21, immediately following the "lex talionis" —"an eye for an eye and a tooth for a tooth," Scripture indicates that a person who by violence inflicts abortion against the will of a prospective mother shall compensate for that fetus by payment of a fine. If the mother's life is lost, the offender will pay with his life in turn. A thing for a thing; a life for a life. The fetus is *not* equated with human life.

In Numbers 5:11-31, if a wife is accused of infidelity, she may be required to drink a potion composed of water and the dust of the tabernacle floor. If sne aborts, as a result, she is judged to have been guilty of adultery. In this event, abortion is mandated by Mosaic law, the priest being the agent of its execution. The point of this is not endorsement of the process, but to demonstrate that the Scriptual understanding of abortion is *not* that of infanticide.

The Talmud attributed humanity to the fetus after the head had emerged from the birth canal. Roman Catholic theology requires baptism of the fetus after it has become "ensouled," so the question of time of "ensoulment" has a long and varied history in the Roman Church. In the Middle Ages, following Aristotelean philosophy, it was assumed that a male fetus was ensouled after 40 days. The female was ensouled at 80 days. In the 13th Century, St. Thomas Aquinas affirmed that upon conception the fetus is a vegetable, later evolving into an animal, and upon two months becomes human. The belief that the fetus is human at conception became dogma quite late in Roman Catholic history. It was at the Vatican Council of 1869 that this was promulgated, along with belief in the infallibility of the Pope and the Assumption of the Virgin (not to be confused, of course, with the Virgin birth).

The reason for this thumb-nail sketch of church history is to assure you that the issue [of abortion] is one of sectarian dogma, a dogma with a short tradition, one without foundation in Scripture, and one that is rejected by the majority of religious denominations in our nation.

Candor requires that I state that the American Roman Catholic bishops, whose authority on the issue of family planning is being rejected by their own constituency, are now stonewalling it on this issue, and are prepared to exert all possible political pressure and to expend immense funds to impose upon the rest of society the findings of their Vatican Council. In strange conjunction, the Vatican position has been endorsed by the political coalition of the moral majority led by Jerry Falwell, which now adds their very considerable resources.

I respect the right of the Roman Church and of others to teach this dogma to their followers, and to use all means of moral persuasion in relation to others. But when they resort to civil law to enforce sectarian dogma upon fellow Americans, I must protest this crass invasion of the rights of conscience and personal freedom. A variety of political ploys have been used to attempt to impose their stance, including the subversion of our American constitution. As one who recognizes the rare and fragile nature of our freedom, I urge you to confirm the Biblical and theological integrity of the position that has been repeatedly affirmed by both streams of our reunited Presbyterian Church (U.S.A.).

Appendix 2
How Papal Authority is Threatened by Population Growth Control

The proposed solutions to the problem of population growth threaten the continued existence of the Catholic Church as it has evolved over the past 2000 years.

It is a matter of public record that the leadership of the Church recognizes this threat and are acting accordingly. Their point of view has been discussed in one of their newspapers, *The National Catholic Reporter,* and in an article reprinted in one of their journals, *Conscience,* in May 1984. According to Thomas Burch, a Georgetown University sociologist and member of the 1966 Papal Commission on Population and Birth Control, the questions put forth to the Commission by the Vatican were quite frank: "(1) Suppose the Vatican changed its mind on contraception. What can we do to present this in such a way that the Church will not lose its moral influence over people? and (2) Suppose the Vatican changed its mind on these issues [population and birth control]. How can we preserve our (the Church's) influence over the marital behavior of individuals?" Of course Professor Burch was shocked by the nature of the Vatican's concerns. The ultimate decision of the Holy See became all too clear with the publication of Humanae Vitae. The Church could not change its position without great loss of authority and power. Instead, this Encyclical initiated the great holy war against family planning now underway.

Unless and until this issue is resolved, there is no hope for population growth control by any humane means. Instead, growth control will be left to the Four Horsemen of the Apocalypse.

The solutions—abortion, family planning, equal rights for women, sex education

—threaten the papacy, the ultimate bastion of the church, because they so seriously undermine the pope's authority. It is important to understand how such measures can be considered threatening. To do so we must examine the history of the Church and the sources of this authority.

Professor Jean-Guy Vaillancourt, a Catholic and a sociologist who has worked in the Vatican for years, devotes a lengthy book, *Papal Power,*[1] published by the University of California Press in 1980, to this subject. Most literate people are aware that Pope John Paul II *has laid papal authority on the line* by repeatedly condemning birth control and abortion, pronouncing many times that neither can ever be justified under any circumstances. Let us first differentiate power, authority and control.

Power is not only actual participation in a decision-making process. Vaillancourt wrote that it is "a capacity to overcome part or all of the resistance, to introduce change in the face of opposition." Power is not necessarily coercive (based on the use of force). It can be persuasive or utilitarian.

"Authority," he observed, "is defined as legitimate power. Authority is not competence or personal influence or leadership. It has to do with legitimate, institutionalized, officially sanctioned power. It is the right to make decisions."

Control is another related concept. According to Vaillancourt, "It can refer to the internalization of norms and values, but it can also refer to power used by one social agent to make another abide by the rules. Social control can be imposed by external force, accepted for economic reasons, or internalized in one's conscience by socialization and by manipulative techniques."

The devastating crisis for the papacy derives from the fact that by legalizing contraception, abortion and other solutions and adopting them as government policy, the authority of the State is visibly pitted against that of the Church:

1   The State is publicly questioning the extent of the Church's legitimate, officially sanctioned power, the very basis of authority.
2   The State is publicly rejecting the claim of papal infallibility.
3   The State is publicly repudiating the Church's claim of the God-given right to be the supreme governor of all men (Pope Pius IX's Syllabus of Errors[2]).

These, together with the ritual of Confession, are the major underpinnings of the basis of control of both laity and clergy. If the general public, through its government, rejects them outright, certainly the authority of the Church will be devastated. A battle to the death between Catholic Church and State is thus underway.

Since the solutions to the population problem (family planning, abortion, etc.) are so popular, and so widely recognized as being absolutely necessary for human survival, there is little doubt who will ultimately prevail. The question remaining is how much suffering and premature death the world will witness in the meantime.

History of the development of papal power

A brief review of Vaillancourt's examination of the history of the development of papal power will clarify these points. As described in *Papal Power,* the Catholic Church's system of control of both laity and clergy is both intricate and highly complex. However, all the external and economic forces at the Vatican's disposal ultimately depend on each individual's conscience, with values internalized by socialization and by manipulative techniques. The Church has spent 2000 years creating this system of controls.

From its inception, the Catholic Church has moved gradually from grass-roots democracy and collegial authority to a vast concentration of power and authority in the hands of clergy and hierarchy, and especially in the hands of the pope and his curia (the central government of the Roman Catholic Church). In the beginning, the Church relied on two sources of power—charismatic and expert. Charismatic power is based on exemplary or ethical prophecy. Examples of this are calls for social justice and equality, maintenance of welfare organizations, establishment of hospitals for the poor and schools for the young, announcements of the "good news," etc. Expert power is based on professional, technical or scientific or purely rational arguments.

Within a few hundred years of its establishment, an alliance developed between Church and State, and Church officials became richer and more powerful. This power might be remunerative (material or nonmaterial rewards), ecological (physical control of material environmental conditions) or coercive (physical and psychic violence). Armed with this strength, these churchmen were able to demand compliance and conformity from the ordinary people.

Traditional power, based on traditional symbols, rituals, magnificent holy edifices, traditional ideas and sentiments, slowly evolved.

A clear-cut administrative-legal structure was developed with the pope at the top and the laity at the bottom. The material wealth and political power of the hierarchy went hand in hand with the disappearance of internal democracy and the increasing use of authoritarian, repressive and manipulative methods of control. The Church became the ideological legitimator of the Roman Empire (as they are for governments of most Catholic countries today). With the fall of the Empire the hierarchy became the religious substitute for the officials of the Empire. The pope came to function as the religious equivalent of the emperor, using some of the techniques of control developed by the Empire. Roman law and Roman administrative procedures, for example, served as models for the development of the Catholic Church's canon law (a source of legal power) and administrative organization. The Church reached its dominance under feudalism.

An internal tension existed in the Church between the functions of legitimization of the feudal order, carried on mostly by the Church hierarchy, and the defense of the oppressed, fulfilled by the lower clergy and lay protesters. This arrangement is easily recognizable in Latin America today, where the hierarchy side with the unresponsive Latin governments which remain entrenched, while the poor are supported by concerned priest and nuns.

During the late feudal period, burning of heretics by the Holy Inquisitions and the Crusaders' holy wars marked the high point of the Church's use of brute force to coerce its followers. With the rise of Protestantism, these methods were frustrated. Alliances with the upper classes of monarchical regimes were preferred to cooperation with the rising masses. However, psychic rather than physical coercion began to be used. Legalism, formalism, obedience, discipline, and the suppression of all remnants of internal democracy became the major preoccupation of Church authorities.

Unable to succeed in this task by themselves, they were increasingly inclined to rely on the help of absolute regimes, and in turn to become the ideological legitimization apparatus for the State. During this period, canon law continued to develop and to be implemented.

In 1801, with the declining influence of those stalwart defenders of the Faith, Spain and Portugal, the Church negotiated a concordat with France, the first of many with different nations, that gave special rights and privileges to the Church in return for ideological legitimization of the governments. These concordats were major sources of Papal strength and influence and continued to be useful in dealing with such leaders as Hitler and Mussolini. Formal and informal agreements with governments continue to be important sources of power.

For centuries the Papal States provided a source of power for the Vatican. They lost them to the patriots who fought to unify Italy. But just before that, in 1870, the first Vatican Council promulgated the dogma of papal infallibility, which dramatically increased the internal power of the Church. The Church has always been flexible, able to accommodate to the inevitable. The hierarchy recognized the spirit of democracy and liberation sweeping around them and wisely saw that they must organize and control democracy by using lay Catholic elites. In 1875, they began to establish Catholic Action groups (social power) which were to defend the rights of the Holy See, and purportedly the religious and social interests of Catholics.

The first political party of Catholic Action in Italy was the Popular Party which was soon disbanded in 1921, as the Pope decided to back the fascist Mussolini in his rise to power. Catholic Action continued to grow and to spread to other countries around the world including the U.S., where it is represented by the Knights of Columbus, Knights of Malta, Opus Dei and other lay organizations. In the 1920's and 1930's, Pius XI negotiated a total of eighteen concordats, a record for any pope. Although he later reversed his attitude toward Mussolini and Hitler, he saw them at first as great men because they were willing to sign a concordat that was advantageous to the Church and they were going to destroy the greatest threat to the Church, communism. Pius XI and his successor Pius XII were hoping for the eventual creation of a mosaic of authoritarian Catholic states in southern Europe. They were counting on traditional forces and on the coercive and legal power of the state to help them retain control of the laity.

After World War II, Pius XII decided to return to the Catholic Party Strategy. He encouraged the creation of the Christian Democratic Party tightly controlled by a centralized Catholic Action movement. These Christian Democratic Parties are found in many countries, including Italy, Germany and El Salvador. In the United States, Catholic Action has not been identified with a single party, because Catholic interests choose candidates for both parties. Since the U.S. National Conference of Catholic Bishop's *Pastoral Plan for Pro-Life Activities* (see Appendix 3) was initiated in 1975, Catholic Action in the United States has been extremely active, protecting Papal interests in the executive, legislative and judicial branches of our government. The Reagan administration has become unquestionably the most Catholic administration in our history. It is a measure of success of the Catholic Action movement in America.

These arrangements between the Vatican and sovereign states necessarily depend on the Church having something to offer governments. This valuable commodity has been the control of large groups of ordinary people and encouragement of their acceptance of the status quo. Through their priests, the Vatican line of class collaboration is stressed, and acceptance of the God-given order of the world as viewed by the Holy See is promulgated. According to ex-Priest Emmett McLoughlin, "It canonizes poverty and insists that men humbly accept their lot in this world as ordained by God and as a test of their worthiness for a better life to come."

The ritual of confession as a source of power

By far the most important mechanism to achieve social control derived from each individual's conscience and his fears is the ritual of Confession. In his book, *Crime & Immorality in the Catholic Church* (New York: Lyle Stuart, 1962), McLoughlin[3] discusses this ritual at length. Throughout the first 1000 years of the Church, confessions were public and much like the Protestant confessions of today. Personal private confession did not become a law of the Church until the year 1216, and was not declared a dogma until 1551. Personal confession slowly developed as an instrument of control and enforcement of discipline. Catholic priests, in their function of hearing confessions, serve as the police force of the hierarchy, watching over all behavior of the believers.

The first confession is one of the most awesome and most sacred events of Roman Catholic childhood, usually taking place at about the age of seven. Frequent confession, required once a month, contributes to the submission to the priesthood.

The elaborate system of sins created by the hierarchy over centuries calls for continuous priestly interpretation and explanation, often making necessary a detailed description of the act of the sin by the confessor. Sins are either venial, such as lying or stealing, which are considered minor sins by Catholic morality, and do not require confession and forgiveness by the priest, or they are mortal, such as fornication or even having a thought about sex. Mortal sins can keep you out of heaven and must be forgiven by a priest.

From early childhood, Catholics are indoctrinated with this system of sin, the concept and intense fear of hell and that priests can forgive their sins. This places enormous power in the hands of priests, who are empowered to keep someone from hell or help some one get to heaven.

The ritual of Confession has several objectives, including, control, fund raising, an opportunity for private indoctrination and to encourage attending Mass every Sunday for public indoctrination.

Control is the most important objective. According to Father McLoughlin, an inordinate emphasis is placed on sins of the flesh in the confessional. These sins usually consume much of the time spent in the confessional. Normal sexual behavior of normal human beings is seized upon by this Catholic system of sins, *insuring that all confessors will have sinned and therefore must submit to the priests' control.* Normal human sexuality is thus exploited and no normal believing human being can escape this exploitation.

The Church guards its authority in all matters dealing with human sexuality. If the State presumes that authority traditionally vested in the Church is actually a government matter, then it can only do so at the expense of the authority (or power) of the Church. The power of the Confessional will be undermined and control of individuals and thus, the masses, will be diminished.

The development of canon law and the claim of papal infallibility have also been essential for keeping the individual Roman Catholic in line. Both are critical to the continued authority of the Church.

Followers are taught that canon law, "God's law," supersedes "man's law" or the law of governments. Breaking a canon law requires absolution by a priest if the follower hopes to make it to heaven. More serious "crimes," such as murdering the pope or abortion (ordinary murder is not such a serious crime), result in automatic "excommunication" which can only be absolved by the pope or his designated representative. Excommunication means that one is blocked from ever entering heaven.

For the devout Catholic who intensely fears hell, excommunication is far worse than death itself. For such an individual, excommunication is the ultimate in psychic coercion, the ultimate act of psychic terrorism. This places tremendous power in the hands of the one who forgives the sin. Probably no more brutal act has ever been conceived for use by one man against another. This threat of excommunication is a very effective weapon to control defenseless individual human beings.

To undermine canon law is to seriously undermine the pope's ability to control his followers through the Confessional. In turn, the pope's bargaining power with governments is vastly reduced, eroding the power he derives from governments.

Many governments are now flatly defying the pope and openly questioning and rejecting his authority by legalizing family planning, abortion, equal rights for women, etc., and even offering these services and promoting them through public policy. The papacy and the Catholic Church as we know them cannot expect to survive this assault on their authority. The Church would have less to offer governments and would in turn derive less power from governments.

Human society subordinated to the purposes of the Church

Where will it all end? It is difficult to predict, but the extinction of the Catholic Church, as we have known it, is possible. The Church leadership recognizes this. The Church does not directly control an army to back up its claims to have the "right to make decisions" that affect all of us. Its claims rest on the intricate and complex set of controls over individuals. If this system is tampered with in any substantive way, then it is subject to possible collapse, as is a building when several pillars are knocked out from under it.

For this reason the Catholic Church has had to stake everything on thwarting State involvement in population growth control, i.e., legalization, participation, policies, etc. The leadership is not concerned with the consequences of their actions, the human misery and premature death that will result. Their guiding principle for the last millennium has been the subordination of society to the purposes of the Church. The ends justify the means.

References

1. Vaillancourt, J.P. 1980. *Papal Power: A Study of Vatican Control Over Lay Catholic Elites.* Berkeley: University of California Press.
2. See Appendix 4 In: Mumford, S.D. 1984. *American Democracy & The Vatican: Population Growth & National Security.* Amherst, New York: Humanist Press.
3. McLoughlin, E. 1962. *Crime & Immorality in the Catholic Church.* New York: Lyle Stuart.

Appendix 3
National Conference of Catholic Bishops' Pastoral Plan for Pro-Life Activities

All should be persuaded that human life and the task of transmitting it are not realities bound up with this world alone. Hence they cannot be measured or perceived only in terms of it, but always have a bearing on the eternal destiny of men.... For God, the Lord of life, has conferred on men the surpassing ministry of safeguarding life in a manner which is worthy of man. Therefore from the moment of its conception life must be guarded with the greatest care, while abortion and infanticide are unspeakable crimes.

—Constitution on the Church in the Modern World

Respect for human life has been gradually declining in our society during the past decade. To some degree this reflects a secularizing trend and a rejection of moral imperatives based on belief in God and His plan for creation. It also reflects a tendency for individuals to give primary attention to what is personally rewarding and satisfying to them, to the exclusion of responsible concern for the well-being of other persons and society. These trends, along with others, have resulted in laws and judicial decisions which deny or ignore basic human rights and moral responsibilities for the protection and promotion of the common good. In this category are efforts to establish permissive

The Bishops' Pastoral Plan, dated November 20, 1975, was produced by the Publications Office, United States Catholic Conference, 1312 Massachusetts Avenue NW, Washington, DC 20005.

abortion laws, the abortion decisions of the United States Supreme Court in 1973 denying any effective legal protection to the unborn child, and the growing attempts to legitimatize positive euthanasia through so-called "death with dignity" laws.

In the Declaration of Independence, our Founding Fathers point to the right to life as the first of the inalienable rights given by the Creator. In fulfillment of our pastoral responsibilities, the members of the National Conference of Catholic Bishops have repeatedly affirmed that human life is a precious gift from God; that each person who receives this gift has responsibilities toward God, toward self, and toward others; and that society, through its laws and social institutions, must protect and sustain human life at every stage of its existence. Recognition of the dignity of the human person, made in the image of God, lies at the very heart of our individual and social duty to respect human life.

In this Pastoral Plan we hope to focus attention on the pervasive threat to human life arising from the present situation of permissive abortion. Basic human rights are violated in many ways: by abortion and euthanasia, by injustice and the denial of equality to certain groups of persons, by some forms of human experimentation, by neglect of the underprivileged and disadvantaged who deserve the concern and support of the entire society. Indeed, the denial of the God-given right to life is one aspect of a larger problem. But it is unlikely that efforts to protect other rights will be ultimately successful if life itself is continually diminished in value.

In focusing attention on the sanctity of human life, therefore, we hope to generate a greater respect for the life of each person in our society. We are confident that greater respect for human life will result from continuing the public discussion of abortion and from efforts to shape our laws so as to protect the life of all persons, including the unborn.

Thus this Pastoral Plan seeks to activate the pastoral resources of the Church in three major efforts:

1. an educational/public information effort to inform, clarify, and deepen understanding of the basic issues;
2. a pastoral effort addressed to the specific needs of women with problems related to pregnancy and to those who have had or have taken part in an abortion;
3. a public policy effort directed toward the legislative, judicial, and administrative areas so as to insure effective legal protection for the right to life.

This Pastoral Plan is addressed to and calls upon all Church-sponsored or identifiably Catholic national, regional, diocesan, and parochial organizations and agencies to pursue the three-fold effort. This includes ongoing dialogue and cooperation between the NCCB/USCC on the one hand, and priests, religious and laypersons, individually and collectively, on the other hand. In a special way we invite the continued cooperation of national Catholic organizations.

At the same time, we urge Catholics in various professional fields to discuss these issues with their colleagues and to carry the dialogue into their own professional organizations. In similar fashion, we urge those in research and academic life to present the Church's position on a wide range of topics that visibly express her commitment to respect for life at every stage and in every condition. Society's responsibility to insure and protect human rights demands that the right to life be recognized and protected as antecedent to and the condition of all other rights.

Dialogue is most important—and has already proven highly fruitful—among Churches and religious groups. Efforts should continue at ecumenical consultation and dialogue with Judaism and other Christian bodies, and also with those who have no specific ecclesial allegiance. Dialogue among scholars in the field of ethics is a most important part of this interfaith effort.

The most effective structures for pastoral action are in the diocese and the parish. While recognizing the roles of national, regional, and statewide groupings, this Plan places its primary emphasis on the roles of diocesan organizations and the parish community. Thus, the resources of the diocese and parish become most important in its implementation.

I. Public Information/Education Program

In order to deepen respect for human life and heighten public opposition to permissive abortion, a two-fold educational effort presenting the case for the sanctity of life from conception onwards is required.

The first aspect, a public information effort, is directed to the general public. It creates an awareness of the threats to human dignity inherent in a permissive abortion policy, and the need to correct the present situation by establishing legal safeguards for the right to life. It gives the abortion issue continued visibility and sensitizes the many people who have only general perceptions of the issue but very little by way of firm conviction or commitment. The public information effort is important to inform the public discussion, and it proves that the Church is serious about and committed to its announced long-range pro-life effort. It is accomplished in a variety of ways, such as accurate reporting of newsworthy events, the issuance of public statements, testimony on legislative issues, letters to editors.

The second aspect, an intensive long-range education effort, leads people to a clearer understanding of the issues, to firm conviction, and to commitment. It is part of the Church's essential responsibility that it carry forward such an effort, directed primarily to the Catholic community. Recognizing the value of legal, medical, and sociological arguments, the primary and ultimately most compelling arguments must be theological and moral. Respect for life must be seen in the context of God's love for mankind reflected in creation and redemption and man's relationship to God and to other members of the human family. The Church's opposition to abortion is based on Christian teaching on the dignity of the human person, and the responsibility to proclaim and defend basic human rights, especially the right to life. This intensive education effort should present the scientific information on the humanity of the unborn child and the continuity of human growth and development throughout the months of fetal existence; the responsibility and necessity for society to safeguard the life of the child at every stage of its existence; the problems that may exist for a woman during pregnancy; and more humane and morally acceptable solutions to these problems.

The more intensive educational effort should be carried on by all who participate in the Church's educational ministry, notably:

- Priests and religious, exercising their teaching responsibility in the pulpit, in other teaching assignments, and through parish programs.
- All Church-sponsored or identifiably Catholic organizations, national, regional, diocesan, and parochial, carrying on continuing education efforts that emphasize the moral prohibition of abortion and the reasons for carrying this teaching into the public policy area.
- Schools, CCD, and other Church-sponsored educational agencies providing moral teaching, bolstered by medical, legal, and sociological data, in the schools, etc. The USCC Department of Education might serve as a catalyst and resource for the dioceses.
- Church-related social service and health agencies carrying on continuing education efforts through seminars and other appropriate programs, and by publicizing programs and services offering alternatives to abortion.

Although the primary purpose of the intensive educational program is the development of pro-life attitudes and the determined avoidance of abortion by each person, the program must extend to other issues that involve support of human life: there must be internal consistency in the pro-life commitment.

The annual Respect Life Program sets the abortion problem in the context of other issues where human life is endangered or neglected, such as the problems facing the family, youth, the aging, the mentally retarded, as well as specific issues such as poverty, war, population control, and euthanasia. This program is helpful to parishes in calling attention to specific problems and providing program formats and resources.

II. Pastoral Care

The Church's pastoral effort is rooted in and manifests her faith commitment. Underlying every part of our program is the need for prayer and sacrifice. In building the house of respect for life, we labor in vain without God's merciful help.

Three facets of the Church's program of pastoral care deserve particular attention.

1. Moral Guidance and Motivation
    Accurate information regarding the nature of an act and freedom from coercion are necessary in order to make responsible moral decisions. Choosing what is morally good also requires motivation. The Church has a unique responsibility to transmit the teaching of Christ and to provide moral principles consistent with that teaching. In regard to abortion, the Church should provide accurate information regarding the nature of the act, its effects and far-reaching consequences, and should show that abortion is a violation of God's laws of charity and justice. In many instances, the decision to do what is in conformity with God's law will be the ultimate determinant of the moral choice.
2. Service and care for women and unborn children
    Respect for human life motivates individuals and groups to reach out to those with special needs. Programs of service and care should be available to provide women with alternate options to abortion. Specifically, these programs should include:

- adequate education and material sustenance for women so that they may choose motherhood responsibly and freely in accord with a basic commitment to the sanctity of life;
- nutritional, pre-natal, childbirth, and post-natal care for the mother, and nutritional and pediatric care for the child throughout the first year of life;
- intensified scientific investigation into the causes and cures of maternal disease and/or fetal abnormality;
- continued development of genetic counseling and gene therapy centers and neo-natal intensive care facilities;
- extension of adoption and foster care facilities to those who need them;
- pregnancy counseling centers that provide advice, encouragement, and support for every woman who faces difficulties related to pregnancy;
- counseling services and opportunities for continuation of education for unwed mothers;
- special understanding, encouragement, and support for victims of rape;
- continued efforts to remove the social stigma that is visited on the woman who is pregnant out of wedlock and on her child.

Many of these services have been and will continue to be provided by Church-sponsored health care and social service agencies, involving the dedicated efforts of professionals and volunteers. Cooperation with other private agencies and increased support in the quest for government assistance in many of these areas are further extensions of the long-range effort.

3. Reconciliation

The Church is both a means and an agent of reconciliation.

Sacramentally, the Church reconciles the sinner through the Sacrament of Penance, thereby restoring the individual to full sacramental participation. The work of reconciliation is also continually accomplished in celebrating and participating in the Eucharist. Finally, the effects of the Church's reconciliating efforts are found in the full support of the Christian community and the renewal of Christian life that results from prayer, the pursuit of virtue, and continued sacramental participation.

Granting that the grave sin of abortion is symptomatic of many human problems, which often remain unsolved for the individual woman, it is important that we realize that God's mercy is always available and without limit, that the Christian life can be restored and renewed through the sacraments, and that union with God can be accomplished despite the problems of human existence.

III. Legislative/Public Policy Effort

In recent years there has been a growing realization throughout the world that protecting and promoting the inviolable rights of persons are essential duties of civil authority, and that the maintenance and protection of human rights are primary purposes of law. As Americans, and as religious leaders, we have been committed to governance by a system of law that protects the rights of individuals and maintains the common good. As our founding fathers believed, we hold that all law is ultimately based on Divine Law, and that a just system of law cannot be in conflict with the law of God.

Abortion is a specific issue that highlights the relationship between morality and law. As a human mechanism, law may not be able fully to articulate the moral imperative, but neither can legal philosophy ignore the moral order. The abortion decisions of the United States Supreme Court (January 22, 1973) violate the moral order, and have disrupted the legal process which previously attempted to safeguard the rights of unborn children. A comprehensive pro-life legislative program must therefore include the following elements:

a) Passage of a constitutional amendment providing protection for the unborn child to the maximum degree possible.

b) Passage of federal and state laws and adoption of administrative policies that will restrict the practice of abortion as much as possible.

c) Continual research into and refinement and precise interpretation of Roe and Doe and subsequent court decisions.

d) Support for legislation that provides alternatives to abortion.

Accomplishment of this aspect of this Pastoral Plan will undoubtedly require well planned and coordinated political action by citizens at the national, state, and local levels. This activity is not simply the responsibility of Catholics, nor should it be limited to Catholic groups or agencies. It calls for widespread cooperation and collaboration. As citizens of this democracy, we encourage the appropriate political action to achieve these legislative goals. As leaders of a religious institution in this society, we see a moral imperative for such political activity.

Means of Implementation of Program

The challenge to restore respect for human life in our society is a task of the Church that reaches out through all institutions, agencies, and organizations. Diverse tasks and various goals are to be achieved. The following represents a systematic organization and allocation of the Church's resources of people, institutions, and finances which can be activated at various levels to restore respect for human life, and insure protection of the right to life of the unborn.

1. State Coordinating Committee

A. It is assumed that overall coordination in each state will be the responsibility of the State Catholic Conference or its equivalent. Where a State Catholic Conference is in process of formation or does not exist, bishops' representatives from each diocese might be appointed as the core members of the State Coordinating Committee.

B. The State Coordinating Committee will be comprised of the Director of the State Catholic Conference and the diocesan Pro-Life coordinators. At this level it would be valuable to have one or more persons who are knowledgeable about public traditions, mores, and attitudes and are experienced in legislative activity. This might be the Public Affairs Specialist referred to under the Diocesan Pro-Life Committee, or, for example, an individual with prior professional experience in legislative or governmental service. In any case, it should be someone with a practical understanding of contemporary political techniques.

C. The primary purposes of the State Coordinating Committee are:

- to monitor the political trends in the state and their implications for the abortion effort;
- to coordinate the efforts of the various dioceses; and to evaluate progress in the dioceses and congressional districts;
- to provide counsel regarding the specific political relationships within the various parties at the state level.

2. The Diocesan Pro-Life Committee

a) General Purpose—The purpose of the Committee is to coordinate groups and activities within the diocese (to restore respect for human life), particularly efforts to effect passage of a constitutional amendment to protect the unborn child. In its coordinating role, the Committee will rely on information and direction from the Bishops' Pro-Life Office and the National Committee for a Human Life Amendment. The Committee will act through the diocesan pro-life director, who is appointed by the bishop to direct pro-life efforts in the diocese.

b) Membership

- Diocesan Pro-Life Director (Bishop's representative)
- Respect Life Coordinator
- Liaison with State Catholic Conference
- Public Affairs Advisor
- Representatives of Diocesan Agencies (Priests, Religious, Lay Organization)
- Legal Advisor—Representative of Pro-Life Groups
- Representatives of Parish Pro-Life Committees
- Congressional District Representative(s)

1. Provide direction and coordination of diocesan and parish education/information efforts and maintain working relationship with all groups involved in congressional district activity.
2. Promote and assist in the development of those groups, particularly voluntary groups involved in pregnancy counseling, which provide alternatives and assistance to women who have problems related to pregnancy.
3. Encourage the development of "grass-roots" political action organization.
4. Maintain communications with National Committee for a Human Life Amendment in regard to federal activity, so as to provide instantaneous information concerning local senators and representatives.
5. Maintain a local public information effort directed to press and media. Include vigilance in regard to public media, seek "equal time," etc.
6. Develop close relationships with each senator or representative.

3. The Parish Pro-Life Committee

The Parish Pro-Life Committee should include a delegate from the Parish Council, representatives of various adult and youth parish organizations, members of local Knights of Columbus Councils, Catholic Daughters of America chapters, and other similar organizations.

Objectives

a) Sponsor and conduct intensive education programs touching all groups within the parish, including schools and religious education efforts.

b) Promote and sponsor pregnancy counseling units and other alternatives to abortion.

c) Through ongoing public information programs generate public awareness of the continuing effort to obtain a constitutional amendment. The NCCB, the National Committee for a Human Life Amendment, and the State and Diocesan Coordinating Committees should have access to every congressional district for information, consultation, and coordination of action. A chairperson should be designated in each district who will coordinate the efforts of parish pro-life groups, K of C groups, etc., and seek ways of cooperating with nonsectarian pro-life groups, including right-to-life organizations. In each district, the parishes will provide one basic resource, and the clergy will have an active role in the overall effort.

d) Prudently convince others—Catholics and non-Catholics—of the reasons for the necessity of a constitutional amendment to provide a base for legal protection for the unborn.

4. The Pro-Life Effort in the Congressional District

Passage of a constitutional amendment depends ultimately on persuading members of Congress to vote in favor of such a proposal. This effort at persuasion is part of the democratic process, and is carried on most effectively in the congressional district or state from which the representative is elected. Essentially, this effort demands ongoing public information activity and careful and detailed organization. Thus it is absolutely necessary to encourage the development in each congressional district of an identifiable, tightly knit, and well-organized pro-life unit. This unit can be described as a public interest group or a citizens' lobby. No matter what it is called:

a) its task is essentially political, that is, to organize people to help persuade the elected representatives; and

b) its range of action is limited, that is, it is focused on passing a constitutional amendment.

As such, the congressional district pro-life group differs from the diocesan, regional, or parish pro-life coordinator or committee, whose task is pedagogic and motivational, not simply political, and whose range of action includes a variety of efforts calculated to reverse the present atmosphere of permissiveness with respect to abortion. Moreover, it is an agency of the citizens. It is not an agency of the Church, nor is it operated, controlled, or financed by the Church.

The congressional district pro-life action group should be bi-partisan, nonsectarian, inclined toward political action. It is complementary to denominational efforts, to professional groups, to pregnancy counseling and assistance groups.

Each congressional district should have a chairperson who may serve as liaison with the Diocesan Coordinating Committee. In dioceses with many congressional districts, this may be arranged through a regional representation structure.

Objectives of the Congressional District Pro-Life Group

1. To conduct a continuing public information effort to persuade all elected officials and potential candidates that abortion must be legally restricted.
2. To counterbalance propaganda efforts opposed to a constitutional amendment.
3. To persuade all residents in the congressional district that permissive abortion is harmful to society and that some restriction is necessary.
4. To persuade all residents that a constitutional amendment is necessary as a first step toward legally restricting abortion.
5. To convince all elected officials and potential candidates that "the abortion issue" will not go away and that their position on it will be subject to continuing public scrutiny.
6. To enlist sympathetic supporters who will collaborate in persuading others.
7. To enlist those who are generally supportive so that they may be called upon when needed to communicate to the elected officials.
8. To elect members of their own group or active sympathizers to specific posts in all local party organizations.
9. To set up a telephone network that will enable the committee to take immediate action when necessary.
10. To maintain an informational file on the pro-life position of every elected official and potential candidate.
11. To work for qualified candidates who will vote for a constitutional amendment and other pro-life issues.
12. To maintain liaison with all denominational leaders (pastors) and all other pro-life groups in the district.

This type of activity can be generated and coordinated by a small, dedicated, and politically alert group. It will need some financial support, but its greatest need is the commitment of other groups who realize the importance of its purposes, its potential for achieving those purposes, and the absolute necessity of working with the group to attain the desired goals.

Conclusion

The challenges facing American society as a result of the legislative and judicial endorsement of permissive abortion are enormous. But the Church and individual Catholics must not avoid the challenge. Although the process of restoring respect for human life at every stage of existence may be demanding and prolonged, it is an effort which both requires and merits courage, patience, and determination. In every age the Church has faced unique challenges calling forth faith and courage. In our time and society, restoring respect for human life and establishing a system of justice which protects the most basic human rights are both a challenge and an opportunity whereby the Church proclaims her commitment to Christ's teaching on human dignity and the sanctity of the human person.

Appendix 4
In God's Name: An Investigation into the Murder of Pope John Paul I (A Summary)

A brief summary of this important book by David A. Yallop (Bantam Books, 1984) follows:

On the afternoon of September 28, 1978, Albino Luciani, formerly Cardinal of Venice, elected Pope John Paul I on August 26, 1978, had a meeting with his Secretary of State, Cardinal Jean Villot, in the Vatican apartments. Having had the opportunity of a month's study of the many problems facing the Papacy, having reviewed the dossiers of the leading members of the Curia, and having instigated a thorough investigation of the Vatican Bank and Vatican finance, Pope John Paul I had decided on startling changes which would affect the doctrine, hierarchy, and finances of the Roman Catholic Church.

Already on September 19 he had informed Cardinal Villot of his disagreement with the stand of Humanae Vitae (Paul VI 1968) on artificial birth control. He directed Villot to respond to the American Embassy that he would receive a U.S. delegation headed by Congressman James Scheuer to discuss this issue and world population on October 24. In 1968, at the request of his superior Cardinal Urbani of Venice, as Bishop Luciani of Vittorio Veneto he had written a report on birth control for Pope Paul VI and the consideration of Vatican II. It recommended that the anovulent pill developed by Professor Pincus should become the Catholic birth control pill.

After discussing a number of new appointments and transfers, the Pope told Villot he was prepared to tackle the difficult problem of the Vatican Bank. Luciani advised Villot that Bishop Marcinkus, its President, was to be removed immediately, the following day. A suitable post in Chicago would be found for him once the problem of Cardinal Cody had been resolved. He would be replaced by Monsignor Abbo, Secretary of the Prefecture of Economic Affairs of the Holy See, an individual with considerable financial experience.

Luciani also made it crystal clear that all links with Michele Sindona and his banks, and Roberto Calvi and Banco Ambrosiano were to be cut in the near future. The Church of Rome was to return to the poor church of its origins. Marcinkus had warned both Sindona and Calvi that an investigation of the Vatican Bank was underway and that he might be removed. Sindona at that time was in New York fighting extradition to Italy. If John Paul I discovered the web of corruption at the Vatican Bank, the track would lead directly to Michele Sindona.

In September 1978 Roberto Calvi was in Buenos Aires conferring with his protector, Licio Gelli, the powerful Grand Master of the secret Masonic organization, P2. In 1971 Licio Gelli arranged the return of General Juan Peron to Argentina from Spain; in 1973 Peron was again President. Roberto Calvi was the "paymaster" of P2, transferring huge amounts on demand to Licio Gelli, the "puppetmaster." His difficulties with Banco Ambrosiano were multiplying, and if the linkage to Vatican Incorporated was revealed, he faced ruin.

The new Pope John Paul I moved next to the "running sore" problem of Cardinal Cody of Chicago in the American Church. He had decided Cody was to be given an ultimatum to resign. He wished inquiries to be made through the Papal Nuncio in Washington about a successor to Cody, and he was concerned that the choice would be a good one. In Chicago, Cardinal Cody received a phone call from Rome: the Pope had decided that Cardinal Cody was to be replaced.

Luciani then advised Villot of a number of other changes he planned to make...and finally that Cardinal Benelli was to become Secretary of State. He would take over Villot's own position.

The discussion with Villot continued for nearly two hours. At 7:30 Villot departed. At 7:50 Luciani sat down to dinner with his two secretaries. At 8:45 he took a phone call from Cardinal Colombo in Milan. Colombo later said, "He spoke to me for a long time in a completely normal tone from which no physical illness could be inferred. He was full of serenity and hope. His final greeting was 'Pray'." At 9:15 he studied a speech briefly which he planned to make to the Jesuits on September 30. At 9:30 he said good night to his two secretaries and closed his study door.

At 4:30 a.m. on September 29 Sister Vincenza carried the container of coffee to the Pope's study as usual and knocked on his bedroom door. For once there was no reply. She returned at 4:45. She knocked again, and noting a light shining from under the door, opened it and saw Albino Luciani sitting up in bed. He was wearing his glasses, and gripped in his hands were some sheets of paper containing the list of appointments and reassignments which he had discussed with Villot the afternoon before. Vincenza felt his pulse. Albino Luciani was dead.

No official death certificate has ever been issued. No autopsy was performed. The cause of death, referred to by the Vatican in the vague terms "possibly related to myocardial infarction," in fact remains unknown. He was embalmed within fourteen hours of a possible time of death when Italian law requires a twenty-four hour waiting period.

The author, David A. Yallop, after three years of intensive investigation, concludes:

"The evidence is all against Luciani's death being natural. The evidence very strongly suggest murder. For myself I have no doubt. I am totally convinced that Albino Luciani was murdered and that at least one of the six suspects I have already identified holds the key."

Villot, Marcinkus, Cody—Gelli, Calvi, Sindona. Each had a great deal to fear if the papacy of John Paul I continued. Whenever or however the plan originated, the implementation of the "Italian Solution" came not a moment too soon. For each of these suspects, a few more days might have been too late.

The tragedy for the Roman Catholic Church and its communicants is that for the second time in a decade the opportunity to open the windows of the Vatican to the fresh air of a more liberal attitude on artificial birth control and other outmoded doctrines of great import to the world was thwarted and lost. With the elevation of Karol Wojtyla as Pope John Paul II it is business as usual at the Vatican. None of Luciani's proposed changes have been implemented. Vatican Incorporated is still functioning in all markets. World and U.S. population continues to expand at exponential growth.

Appendix 5
An Example of the Taboo
on the Discussion of Conspiracy

Possibly the most far-reaching Vatican political conspiracy in American history was described in a book written in 1963 by ex-priest Emmett McLoughlin, *An Inquiry into the Assassination of Abraham Lincoln*, published by Lyle Stuart, New York. Why would anyone wish to assassinate America's revered President Abraham Lincoln? McLoughlin presents these facts:

1. Pope Pius IX and Abraham Lincoln were contemporaries for fifty-six years.
2. In the early 1860s the alignment of forces was clear. On one side were dictatorship, slavery, secession: monarchy in the form of Emperor Franz Joseph of Austria, Emperor Napoleon III of France, and King Leopold of Belgium who conspired to place Hapsburg Archduke Maximilian on the throne of Mexico as Emperor; European Imperialism, Jesuit chicanery, and a Catholic Church dominated assault upon the Monroe Doctrine, all of which found spiritual leadership in the one person, Pope Pius IX.

   On the other side were the ideas of freedom, emancipation, Freemasonry, democracy, Latin American struggles against foreign domination, all embodied in one person, Abraham Lincoln.

   The monarchies and the Vatican sided with the South during the Civil War. They hoped its victory and that of Maximilian would enhance the political power of the Vatican throughout North America.
3. The Syllabus of Errors of Pope Pius IX (80) contains the following: #20 The

ecclesiastical power has a right to exercise its authority independent of the toleration or assent of the civil government. #25 The temporal power which is...conceded as belonging to the Episcopacy . . . is not revocable at the pleasure of the civil authority. #55 The Church ought to be in union with the State, and the State with the Church. (His complete Syllabus of 80 Errors can be found in Appendix 4 of Ref. 37.)

4. Of the ten conspirators, John Wilkes Booth, the trigger man, was killed; John H. Surratt, his major accomplice, had studied for the Catholic priesthood in St. Charles College, Maryland, before becoming a Confederate spy and courier; he escaped to Canada, England, and Rome under Church sanctuary and was hidden for a year in the Zouave Guards of the Vatican; discovered, he was returned to Washington, treated to a long, expensive trial which ended in two hung juries and finally was included in President Johnson's general pardon in November 1868. Throughout his trial and afterward he had the support of Catholic attorneys and the Jesuits of Georgetown College. Of the remaining eight, four were sentenced to death by hanging, three to life imprisonment, and one to six years imprisonment.

5. The conspiracy included not only the assassination of President Lincoln, but also of Vice President Andrew Johnson, Secretary of State Seward, and the victorious Union General Ulysses S. Grant. Seward was stabbed by Lewis Paine but lived. Johnson was saved because George Atzerodt got drunk and lost his nerve. General Grant had fortunately left town. All analysts agree that the conspiracy could not have been planned and carried out by the abilities of the conspirators themselves. Higher motivation, direction, and resources were required.

6. Seven of the ten conspirators were Roman Catholic. Booth was Catholic. Mary Surratt, mother of John Surratt, ran the boardinghouse where the conspirators met and was a devout and fanatical Catholic. Five priests testified in her behalf at her trial.

Special Judge Advocate John A. Bingham quoted in "The Trial of the Conspirators," Washington, 1865, as cited by McLoughlin

"A conspiracy is rarely, if ever, proved by positive testimony. . . . Unless one of the original conspirators betrays his companions and gives evidence against them, their guilt can be proved only by circumstantial evidence. It is said by some writers on evidence that such circumstances are stronger than positive proof. A witness swearing positively may misapprehend the facts or swear falsely, but that circumstances can not lie."